The Migraine Relief Diet

The Migraine Relief Diet

Meal Plan and Cookbook for Migraine Headache Reduction

TARA SPENCER

ROCKRIDGE PRESS

Foreword

M any people aren't aware of how common migraines are. Three out of every 100 men, and 1 out of every 10 women suffer from migraine headaches. The largest numbers of sufferers are 30–40 years old, when they are typically busiest with families and careers.

What happens when migraines occur, and how are they triggered? It's believed that if you have migraine disease, you have one or more genes affecting how your nervous system works. Although there are many different forms of migraine disease, the common feature is that your nervous system is more sensitive than normal. When your nerves are stimulated, a reaction deep in the brain causes electrical activity and the release of chemicals that cause blood vessels to dilate and constrict. The inflammation causes swelling and pain. But this exaggerated response can set off other parts of the nervous system that are not causing pain. This explains why migraine attacks include temporary intestinal effects, usually nausea and vomiting, and visual effects, such as wavy lines and blind spots. It also explains temporary inability to speak, numbness, or even paralysis of any body part. And, after the headache, there is a lingering day or two of confused thinking, light sensitivity, and fatigue.

Your migraine disease usually changes with time. It may have caused colic or vomiting in infancy, carsickness as a youth, or traditional headaches as a teenager, and dizziness as an adult. With hormonal changes and the lasting effects of repeated brain inflammation, many people with migraine headaches evolve into more daily symptoms of facial pressure, skin sensitivity, and other odd sensations. It is believed that by controlling the triggers of migraine attacks, you might be able to avoid the more chronic form of the disease.

Triggers can be any environmental, dietary, or physiologic factor. Common environmental triggers include weather changes, a painful stimulus, strong odors, and excessive light or noise. Physiologic triggers include lack of sleep, stress, and hormonal changes. There may be more than one way our body reacts negatively to what we eat. Some speculate that some by-products from absorbed food molecules penetrate the nervous system and mimic neurotransmitters or directly provoke the nervous system. These are chemical triggers. But there is another indirect way that foods trigger the nervous system—for some migraineurs, they react to a food ingredient as a foreign body and it sets off an immune system response.

There are hundreds of potential food triggers for migraines. Comprehensive lists of foods that may contribute to triggering migraine can be found online, though some are provided within the following pages. How and why some people react so abnormally to different food proteins or chemicals is not yet well understood.

In general, food triggers fall into three main categories:

1. By-products of food aging and fermentation (red wine, aged cheeses)
2. Foods with chemicals similar to neurotransmitters our brains use (coffee, chocolate, MSG, and the nitrates found in cured meats)
3. Foods to which we have mild, or silent, allergies or sensitivities

Frequently a migraine patient will be tested for an allergy, and an allergic sensitivity to a common food will be found. Even when the food does not cause gastrointestinal distress, which typically suggests intolerance, elimination of the food item from the diet is often found to be helpful. Sometimes a food allergy can be identified by skin and blood tests. For example, blood testing can identify an allergy to gluten, called celiac disease, but the majority of people who have some other form of sensitivity to the proteins in grains cannot be recognized with a blood test.

The use of an elimination diet— a careful removal of specific foods over a period of time, followed by a reintroduction of the food—is one of the most reliable methods to identify a dietary migraine trigger. Use this book as your guide through the steps of an elimination diet, then through the reintroduction phase, to help you identify your dietary triggers.

Above all, be patient. It may take 6-10 weeks before you see any improvement, but most people do. After an improvement in symptoms is achieved, suspect foods can be added back to the diet one at a time to identify triggers. Despite the difficulty of this kind of a trial, we have found that even the most severely affected migraineurs tend to respond, and are generously rewarded for their efforts. The migraine-safe recipes in this book can help you identify a new way to control your migraine disease. We hope this material will help you achieve better control of your migraine symptoms, and improve your quality of life.

—Frederick Godley, III, MD, FACS, President of the Association of Migraine Disorders and
Michael Teixido, MD, Vice President of the Association of Migraine Disorders

Preface

A *migraine* is a complex neurological disorder afflicting about 15 percent of the world's population. I experienced my first migraine at the age of five. Doctors dismissed my complaints despite the fact that I exhibited all the classic migraine symptoms: pain at the temples, severe pressure in the head, and acute sensitivity to light and noise. In addition, I was genetically predisposed to migraines. Nevertheless, I was told that I was too young to be a *migraineur*—someone who suffers from migraines. My migraines increased in severity and frequency, and yet I was still unable to obtain a proper diagnosis until I was 10 years old. Until then, it was a difficult time for my childhood self, who was given no explanation as to why it felt as though her brain was attempting to burst through her skull.

Growing up, I watched my father endure regular attacks, which usually rendered him to tears. I learned that some of his triggers also applied to me, but also that my own migraines were different in many ways. For example, we were both affected by similar foods and loud noises, but he didn't share my sensitivity to lights and smells. As a child, my migraines were worse than what I have experienced so far as an adult; back then, they were almost always accompanied by vomiting—a symptom I have largely managed to escape in recent years.

I suffered from regular attacks for almost 20 years. At my worst, I experienced at least one migraine per week over a two-year period, which seriously affected both my professional and social life. Frequently, I was forced to take sick days or cut my workdays short. At that time I was working in the finance industry, which is known for its long hours and high stress levels—the latter of which is widely recognized as a migraine trigger. Because I was missing so many hours of work, I found myself becoming even more stressed, and the vicious cycle continued.

Like many people, I resigned myself to the idea that migraines were an unavoidable part of my life. Sadly, weekly attacks became my version of normal. My body never responded to any type of medication, and other lifestyle factors commonly cited as natural means of relief—such as exercise and massage—granted very temporarily relief.

In 2012, I became a certified nutritionist. I put my newfound knowledge to use and took control of my own diet in an attempt to manage my migraines. Certain foods such as processed meats and caffeine had always been bad triggers for me, but I was largely unaware of the wider range of potentially triggering foods in existence. When I eliminated all these foods, in conjunction with addressing other lifestyle factors, I managed to reduce my migraine frequency and severity dramatically. Thankfully, I was able to reintroduce some of those trigger foods at a later stage, but I was ready to accept a more restrictive diet if it meant being pain-free and functional. As with many medical problems, symptoms and treatment vary on a case-by-case basis, so personal experimentation and close monitoring is key.

In the past year I have had three migraine events, and each time I was able to alleviate the pain via over-the-counter medication. I no longer suffer from frequent neck and shoulder pain that precedes an inevitable migraine, and I am less paranoid that every bright light and strong smell will set off an attack. All of this would have been unfathomable during the time when I was afflicted by more than 50 migraines per year and unresponsive to the strongest of prescription medication. Modifying my diet to avoid trigger foods has made me feel significantly healthier, and doing so has drastically increased my quality of life.

Although migraines cannot be cured completely, they can be managed. Most long-term migraine sufferers have tried every standard method, including taking pain-relieving medications as well as preventive medications. However, it is common for sufferers to show resistance to traditional medicine. As someone's predisposition toward migraines is usually revealed in childhood or early adolescence, many simply accept that they are doomed to a life of untreatable attacks. It does not have to be that way.

The Migraine Relief Diet addresses frustrations with the body's lack of response to traditional treatment methods. It is for those who desire to find a more natural means to heal their bodies, primarily via dietary changes. This book is for those who have never considered a dietary change as a method of healing or have perhaps tried but gone about it the wrong way. Processed foods, dairy, sugar, artificial sweeteners, caffeine, and alcohol are frequently assumed to be migraine triggers, as are undereating and meal skipping. This book will teach you how to best structure your nutritional approach to dramatically reduce your incidence of migraines by first eliminating and then later reintroducing the aforementioned inflammatory foods.

The Migraine Relief Diet provides you with a complete dietary template to follow for 28 days, alongside recipes, to ensure the transition is as simple and delicious as possible. With tasty recipes to choose from for every meal, you will hardly notice that you have eliminated certain foods. At the end of the month, you can customize the diet according to your personal tastes and soon-to-be-revealed triggers. *The Migraine Relief Diet* will help you begin a new, healthy chapter of your life.

A migraine is a complicated medical disorder with a list of symptoms that varies from person to person. Despite its prevalence in society, migraine disorder is still largely misunderstood. The first part of this book will explore the medical definition of the condition, considering how and why migraines occur. I will discuss the standard medical interventions that are employed to treat migraines, as well as some alternative natural healing options.

The first part will also explore some of the common triggers for migraines—including food—and explain how they can combine to cross an individual's threshold, thereby leading to a migraine attack. I will show you that the best way to reduce the frequency and intensity of your migraine episodes is to employ a whole-body approach by taking time to exercise, eat healthily, avoid triggers, and find suitable methods of stress relief.

PART

1

UNDERSTANDING MIGRAINES

Chapter One

A Complex Disorder

A number of well-known figures throughout history have suffered from migraines, including Charles Darwin, Albert Einstein, Sigmund Freud, and Vincent van Gogh. Emily Dickinson even wrote about her migraine experiences in her poem "I Felt a Funeral, in My Brain." Whoopi Goldberg, Janet Jackson, Hugh Jackman, Lisa Kudrow, and Serena Williams are contemporary migraineurs. Many of these celebrities have spoken publicly about their condition, and revealed that it has negatively affected their work at times.

It is estimated that as many as half of all migraineurs suffer in silence without seeking medical intervention. Hence, the exact statistic of sufferers is unknown, but it is believed to be somewhere between 12 and 22 percent of the population. According to recent figures from Migraine.com, in the United States, almost five million people experience at least one migraine per month, with more than 37 million people overall reportedly suffering from the disorder.

According to researchers, women are three times more likely than men to suffer from migraines, and about one in four women will experience migraines during their reproductive years (Smitherman et al., 2013). Attacks are closely linked to hormonal fluctuations, which occur during women's monthly menstrual cycles. This also means that the frequency and severity of women's attacks can alter during pregnancy and menopause, and can be exacerbated by hormonal contraceptive methods.

About 70 percent of people who experience migraines have a family history of the disorder. Migraine frequency is believed to peak between early and middle adulthood and decline substantially thereafter. As many as 10 percent of children under the age of 15 will suffer from migraines, which will more than likely continue into adulthood (Migraine.com).

In this chapter we will define what a migraine is and what it is not, and teach you strategies for tracking your migraine events. If you have been suffering for a long time, you have probably already done your research and likely also sought medical intervention, so the information in this chapter may not be entirely new for you. It is, however, crucial to briefly address how and why migraines occur so that we can attempt to recognize and halt them during the early stages. From there, we will look at the standard treatment methods and then consider the ways food can be used to control your migraines.

What Is a Migraine?

A migraine is a condition brought on by abnormal activity in the brain, usually in the form of excessive firing of nerves. It is most commonly recognized as an extremely painful headache frequently accompanied by nausea, vomiting, blurred vision, and heightened sensitivity to light, sound, and smell. This head pain is often pulsating or isolated in one location, usually around one of the temples or behind one of the eyes.

However, it is important to note that migraines do not always involve head pain. Although it is common, migraine is about much more than head pain. Many people experience migraines as dizziness, facial pain and pressure, and/or nasal congestion. These symptoms can also vary over a lifetime.

Migraines can be debilitating, wiping sufferers out for up to 72 hours at a time. There is no normalcy with regard to episode frequency between sufferers: Some people experience a few migraines per year, while others suffer from several each month.

Migraines put a strain on the medical system. Beyond the burden of the migraine itself, they are associated with increased rates of medical and psychiatric comorbidities. Data from the Centers for Disease Control and Prevention (2014) indicates that headache is among the top five reasons for emergency department visits and among the top 20 reasons for outpatient medical visits in the United States. About one in four migraineurs reported visiting the emergency room due to severe head pain.

According to data from the American Migraine Study II (Lipton et al., 2001), 73 percent of people experience nausea, and 29 percent vomit during a migraine. Furthermore, those who suffer from migraine-related nausea report more severe pain and greater difficulties obtaining relief via medication.

Most people cannot work or function normally during a migraine attack, with the average sufferer missing two days of work each year. As migraines are more prominent during the most productive working years of one's life, the disorder takes a clear financial toll. According to the American Headache Society (2015), lost work due to migraines costs the United States more than $13 billion each year. The public health impact of the disorder will continue to be a major problem for society unless something can be done to improve treatment methods.

Let's take a look at the four common stages of a migraine:

- Prodrome
- Aura
- Attack
- Postdrome

It's important to note that not everyone will experience each stage: Many simply suffer from the headache itself, while others may only experience the nonheadache symptoms.

Prodrome

The *prodrome* phase occurs anywhere between one hour and two days before a migraine strikes, and includes symptoms such as mood changes, constipation, food cravings, neck stiffness, and uncontrollable yawning. While most will feel depressed and irritable, others will feel hyperactive and happy. These symptoms may simply be indicative of other conditions, so migraineurs may have to use their own judgment to determine whether a migraine is on its way.

Aura

For around one in three migraineurs who suffer from severe head pain, their attacks are sometimes preceded or accompanied by what is known as *aura*. A symptom of the nervous system, aura includes seeing flashing lights and experiencing tingling in the extremities as well as speech or language difficulties. Each of these symptoms usually lasts for 20 to 60 minutes.

WHERE MIGRAINES LIVE

Despite their prevalence, migraines are still one of the most poorly understood medical disorders. Most people assume that a migraine involves a headache, but we now know that is not necessarily the case. A definitive cause of migraines has not yet been discovered, largely because most people vary dramatically in their reported causes and symptoms. For a long time, they were believed to be caused by problems with the blood vessels in the head; however, it is now understood that migraines are a disorder of the central nervous system.

Although the exact chain of physical and chemical events that occurs in the brain in advance of a migraine is unclear, it appears that migraines are sometimes caused by changes in the brain stem and its interactions with the body's largest cranial nerve and its major pathway to pain, the *trigeminal nerve*. Sometimes, they may be caused by imbalances in brain chemicals—predominantly *serotonin*, which helps regulate pain in the body as well as control mood, sleep, and appetite. Serotonin levels drop during migraine attacks, which may cause the trigeminal nerve to release *neuropeptides*—the molecules through which neutrons communicate with one another. These neuropeptides then travel to the *meninges*—the protective membrane covering the brain—resulting in headache pain.

Within about 10 minutes, the pain-sensing nerves in this network become hypersensitive to pressure. They are so sensitive, they become affected by the natural rise and fall of blood pressure occurring during each heartbeat, which produces the feeling of throbbing pain within the head. Alongside these changes, an unknown factor seems to contribute to the dilation of blood vessels, which in turn produces abnormal activity at the surface of the brain.

> " *I have had a long history with migraines. Early on, I identified triggers such as secondhand cigarette smoke; then, later, alcohol, caffeine, stress, sudden changes in barometric pressure, and hormonal fluctuations. In the last two years, I've seen remarkable results by avoiding sugar, dairy, and gluten, and eating primarily organic foods. It's been a long road, but I'm grateful to be on this side of understanding and controlling my condition.* "
>
> —Lori, nurse, age 54

While most migraine sufferers do not experience aura, there is no guarantee that those who do can delay or prevent the onset of a severe headache by the time the aura presents. Oftentimes, auras only act as a warning that the sufferer will soon have to ride out their pain in a dark, quiet room.

Attack

The migraine itself occurs during the *attack* stage, the most acute of the stages. A migraine will typically last from 4 to 72 hours if left untreated. While not every sufferer will experience head pain, those who do may feel pain on both sides of the head or, more commonly, just one side—and it may also switch sides. The pain may be pulsating or throbbing. It may cause nausea and/or vomiting, and this is closely tied to an extreme sensitivity to lights, sounds, and smells. Sufferers' vision may blur (this can also occur as part of the aura stage), and they may feel light-headed, which can even lead to fainting.

The attack stage may also lack the presence of a headache itself but may instead involve nausea, vertigo, ear pain and pressure, sinus pressure and congestion, anxiety, seizures, irritable bowels, or bladder pain. These episodes are diagnosed as migraines, even without head pain.

Postdrome

Postdrome is the final stage of a migraine, where the sufferer will experience changes in mood and feelings. This stage is often likened to a hangover. Most people will feel fatigued and light-headed during this period; however, others report feelings of euphoria.

On the Migraine Spectrum

As a migraine is more than just the headache most people think of, and symptoms vary greatly from person to person, it is difficult to pin down exactly what a migraine is not. That said, many people mistakenly believe that a migraine is simply a recurring bad headache that can be fixed by popping a few painkillers; in fact, the majority of headaches are not migraines. As explained earlier, a migraine is a severe, debilitating condition with a clear set of symptoms that do not occur alongside regular headaches. Finally, many migraines do not even involve the presence of severe head pain.

Regular headaches can successfully be treated with standard medicine or rest, and they do not typically last for longer than a day. There are different types of headaches, but they are not as serious as migraines as they generally do not interfere with productivity and quality of life. Other headaches may present like migraines but in actuality be either a tension headache or a cluster headache. Increasingly, however, physicians believe the following are extremes on the migraine spectrum—what separates these from what we think of as "true" migraines is that they are typically unaffected by dietary changes.

Tension Headaches

Tension headaches are the most common type of headache, with an estimated 80 to 90 percent of the population suffering from at least one in their lifetime (American Headache Society). Characterized by a dull ache, tension headaches are typically caused by muscle tension, caffeine withdrawal, lack of sleep, or dehydration. The pain typically occurs throughout the head, across the forehead, or at the base of the neck and is generally rated as mild to moderate in severity. These recurrent headaches can last anywhere from minutes to days.

Cluster Headaches

Cluster headaches are commonly distinguished by a sudden and severe pain behind or around the eye, which typically peaks within 10 minutes but can last up to three hours. They can be accompanied by other symptoms such as watering eyes, nasal congestion, and swelling around the side of the eye where pain is being experienced.

The main difference between these types of headaches and a migraine is that the former usually respond to over-the-counter pain relievers. None of the symptoms associated with migraines such as aura, nausea, and sensory sensitivity are present with these other types of headaches.

Triggers and Thresholds

There are two important factors to consider regarding the onset of migraines: triggers and thresholds. A *trigger* is an external stimulus or physical act that increases the sensitivity of the sensory system and can result in a migraine. Some of these sensors are "external" and affect the olfactory, auditory, and ocular nerves which, in turn, explains a migraineur's potential sensitivity to smell, noise, and lights, respectively. The "internal" sensors are thought to be located within the brainstem, and are those that react to fatigue, stress, hormonal, and barometric pressure.

The brains of migraineurs have been shown to have a poor ability to adapt to strong sensory stimulation, which is why these triggers do not cause negative reactions in all people. Because of the accompanying chemical changes that occur inside the body during a migraine, being exposed to triggers does not always result in migraines. This is where the idea of a migraine *threshold* comes into play.

Everyone has a threshold, which is determined by genetic makeup. This threshold is raised or lowered by both internal and external factors. When a sufficient number of different internal and external triggers build up, a migraineur's threshold may be crossed, resulting in a migraine.

Triggers

The following are common contributing factors to migraines. Remember that exposure to just one of the following may not always be sufficient to cause an attack.

Alcohol Alcohol can cause two different types of migraine. The first occurs when you experience a more immediate attack, occurring within a few hours of drinking. The second is a delayed hangover-type headache; many people develop a headache after a night of heavy drinking, but the pain is intensified in migraineurs. Those who report alcohol to be a trigger only need the smallest amount to be affected, so it is best to abstain.

Bright Lights Many people are negatively affected by bright light such as fluorescent and strobe lighting and sun glare as well as flickering sunlight.

66 Starting at age eight, my migraines were episodic until my mid to late twenties, when the condition became chronic. I still live with the disorder. Four years ago I stopped using prescription medications due to their side effects and ineffectiveness. I manage my pain through the use of a neurostimulator, Botox injections, and natural pain relief methods. I avoid my individual food triggers (alcohol, peanuts, and popcorn, among others) and exclude dairy, soy, gluten, and processed foods from my diet. 99

—Valerie, age 37, Virginia

Caffeine Highly caffeinated beverages are closely tied to migraine episodes. Most people have heard about the horrible headaches that can occur when a regular person suffers caffeine withdrawals, due to its addictive properties. As you might imagine, these headaches can be significantly worse for migraineurs.

In some cases, caffeine can be strategically used to prevent an oncoming migraine during the prodrome or aura stage. Many pain-relieving medications contain caffeine, and even a shot of espresso can help. This is because caffeine constricts cranial blood vessels, which counteracts the dilation effect that usually causes a migraine. Furthermore, it enhances the absorption of other medications.

Personally, when I suffered from more regular attacks, I could prevent an episode by drinking coffee if I recognized the oncoming signs of a migraine early enough. It worked well as I never consumed caffeine outside of these times.

Computer Screens Using a computer for long periods of time can be problematic for migraineurs, both due to the strain on the eyes and the buildup of muscular tension in the neck and shoulders.

Dehydration Even mild dehydration can cause migraines, so it is important to ensure you drink at least eight glasses of water per day. Caffeine and alcohol also have a dehydrating effect, so you should be all the more careful about consuming them.

Environmental Extremes Severe heat and other extremes in weather, including changes in barometric pressure, are thought to cause migraines. There is not much that can be done to avoid these triggers; however, certain preventive treatments can help reduce your sensitivity to these factors.

Foods While this will be discussed in significantly more detail in part 2 of this book, it is widely accepted that salty and processed foods, aged cheeses and other dairy products, fermented and pickled foods, and foods containing the additive tyramine (such as soy products, fava beans, sausages, and smoked fish) often cause migraines. The sweetener aspartame and the preservative monosodium glutamate (MSG) are also widely thought to trigger migraines. Even certain types of fruits and vegetables are recognized as triggers.

High Stress Levels A sudden increase in stress at home or at work will alter the chemicals in your body and increase muscle tension, both of which frequently lead to migraines. Interestingly enough, the converse is also true as a sudden reduction in stress can cause an attack. For example, it is not unusual to be struck down by a migraine on the weekend or when you go on vacation.

Hormonal Fluctuations Estrogen fluctuations during a normal menstrual cycle are often strongly linked to migraine patterns among females. Women with histories of migraines typically report attacks occurring before or during their periods, when they experience a major drop in estrogen. Many women also report that their suffering began at puberty, with the onset of their first period (The Migraine Trust, 2015).

Those women who already experience migraines often report an increase in their intensity of attacks during both pregnancy and menopause. In addition, women who have never previously had a history of migraines can be suddenly stricken during these two moments of significant hormonal change.

Skipping Meals Missing meals or fasting will cause blood sugar levels to drop, which can in turn trigger migraines. Similarly, frequently eating sugary snacks instead of proper meals will create peaks and valleys in your blood sugar levels.

Sleep There is a strong correlation between sleep and migraines. Although it may seem obvious that sleeping too little can bring about migraines, sleeping too much can also be problematic. New sleep schedules and jet lag can also trigger migraines. Those who suffer from migraines often report having difficulty falling asleep and frequently waking up feeling tired.

Unusual Smells The most common smells thought to spark migraines include perfume, secondhand smoke, air freshener, and paint thinner.

Threshold

As mentioned previously, a combination of the aforementioned triggers can accumulate past your threshold and result in a migraine. This explains why certain triggers do not always cause migraines on their own or in various combinations. For example, your three worst triggers may be red wine, bright sunshine, and lack of sleep, but one of those triggers on its own may not be enough to provoke a migraine. If all three occur simultaneously, however, you may be more likely to cross your threshold.

By identifying your most problematic triggers, you can better avoid reaching your own personal threshold and thereby reduce the frequency of your migraine attacks. It is important to keep in mind that individual thresholds will vary from day to day and from environment to environment, and some days you will be more vulnerable to certain triggers.

Common Medical Interventions for Migraines

When you are diagnosed as a migraineur, your doctor will typically prescribe medications based on the severity of your symptoms as well as any other health conditions you have. Over-the-counter medicines will rarely provide relief.

Of course, there are always risks involved in relying on medication. Furthermore, taking any of these medicines for more than 10 days out of a 30-day period, for longer than 3 months, can cause more headaches due to medication overuse.

Medications prescribed to migraine sufferers fall into one of two categories. *Pain-relieving medications* are taken during attacks—ideally during the prodrome or aura stage—and are designed to stop symptoms from progressing further. *Preventive medications* are taken regularly, usually on a daily basis, to reduce the severity and/or frequency of migraine episodes.

Pain-Relieving Medications

Pain-relieving medications include aspirin and nonsteroidal anti-inflammatory drugs (NSAIDs) such as ibuprofen. The most common antimigraine analgesic is *triptan*, with nearly half of those prescriptions being for sumatriptan (Imitrex). Triptans work by promoting the constriction of blood vessels in the brain while simultaneously blocking pain pathways. This counteracts the blood vessel dilation that is thought to be a contributing factor to the development of migraines.

Ergots *Ergots*, such as Migranal and Cafergot, are combination drugs containing ergotamine and caffeine. (While caffeine itself is a common trigger, it can also be preventive when used strategically.) They are sometimes prescribed as they prevent the dilation of blood vessels, which causes migraines, and they are most effective in those whose pain usually lasts longer than 48 hours. Ergots have been shown to be less effective than triptans in head-to-head trials and are typically only effective if taken in the early stages of a migraine. Ergots often worsen the nausea and vomiting related to migraines and are dangerous due to the high risk of poisoning, which can lead to gangrene, vision problems, unconsciousness, and even death.

Opioid Medications For those who cannot take triptans or ergots, *opioid medications* containing narcotics—usually codeine—are sometimes prescribed. Opioid medications are highly addictive and can cause drowsiness, constipation, sleep apnea, and heart and lung problems. They are generally only used as a last resort.

Preventive Medications

Preventive medications are usually prescribed to those who suffer from two or more migraines per month, which do not generally respond to pain-relieving medication, and to those who experience attacks lasting more than 12 hours. These drugs not only help prevent the onset of migraines but also make the body more responsive to pain-relieving medications.

Doctors may prescribe a daily medication or something to be taken only when a predictable trigger, such as menstruation, is approaching. These preventive drugs—including antidepressants, antiseizure drugs, and cardiovascular drugs—are potentially more dangerous than pain-relieving medications as they can cause a number of serious side effects.

SEROTONIN SYNDROME

Many of the medications prescribed to improve migraines work by boosting the amount of serotonin in the brain, which subsequently increases your risk of developing the rare and potentially life-threatening condition, "serotonin syndrome." This condition makes one prone to hallucinations, nausea, vomiting, diarrhea, and an increased heart rate.

Serotonin syndrome can be caused by taking triptans and antidepressants known as *selective serotonin reuptake inhibitors (SSRIs) or serotonin and norepinephrine reuptake inhibitors (SNRIs).*

Common SSRIs include sertraline (Zoloft), fluoxetine (Sarafem, Prozac), and paroxetine (Paxil), while SNRIs include duloxetine (Cymbalta) and venlafaxine (Effexor XR).

Antidepressants Certain *antidepressants* can help prevent migraines by altering the level of serotonin and other chemicals within the brain, but they also commonly cause mouth dryness, constipation, and weight gain.

Antiseizure Drugs *Antiseizure* drugs are also commonly prescribed to migraine sufferers, yet they can cause nausea, diarrhea, tremor, weight gain, hair loss, and dizziness.

Botox For those who do not tolerate traditional migraine medication well, there is one alternative for chronic sufferers. *Botox*, or onabotulinum toxin A, is well known for smoothing out wrinkles, but it is also linked to treating chronic migraines in adults. In 2010, the US Food and Drug Administration approved the drug as a treatment option for those who suffer migraines for 15 days or more each month. Botox is not thought to grant any benefits to nonchronic sufferers.

When used as a treatment option, multiple Botox injections are made into the forehead and neck every 12 weeks. These injections help prevent or dull future symptoms associated with the headache portion of the migraine episode. It can take up to 14 days to witness any kind of improvement, and some people require multiple treatments before they experience any relief.

The major risks of Botox include neck pain and further headaches and, in rare cases, muscle weakness and vision problems.

Cardiovascular Drugs *Cardiovascular drugs*, like beta-blockers and calcium channel blockers, can be very effective in preventing migraines and relieving symptoms during attacks; however, they often cause fatigue, digestive problems, dizziness, and shortness of breath.

MIGRAINE DIARY

To determine which of the aforementioned triggers are applicable to you, you should keep a diary of your attacks. By using the following template, you will be able to identify any patterns among the factors that coincide with your attacks. This diary is available for download at callistomedia.com/migrainereliefdiet.

Date and day of the week

What time did the migraine start?

How long did the migraine last?

Did you do anything to treat it? Did it work?

What were you doing leading up to the attack?

How many hours did you sleep the previous night?

What did you eat in the 24 hours prior to the attack?

What medications were you taking at the time?

Have you recently experienced any major life changes or stresses?

Chapter Two

A Whole-Body Approach

You can use strategies in tandem with medical intervention to help abate migraines. While medication can help prevent migraines from occurring or reduce the pain involved in an attack, you must consider your body as a whole. The human body was designed to fight off illness and infection without the help of drugs. Ailments can be cured through your diet, and by ensuring you are treating your body with love and care by participating in activities that promote optimal health.

Mitigating your risk of migraine attacks is not only about avoiding triggers, but also taking part in health-boosting activities such as exercise, yoga, and meditation. As part of your full-body approach to treating your migraines, you may also wish to consider alternative methods of treatment such as acupuncture, aromatherapy, biofeedback, cognitive behavioral therapy, and massage therapy.

The following strategies will help you either cut down on the number of migraine events you experience per month or dial them down in the prodrome or aura stage.

Avoid Triggers

Although medical treatments for migraines are readily available, in an ideal world we would be able to prevent migraines from occurring in the first place by identifying and steering clear of triggers. The best thing you can do to reduce your incidence of migraine attacks is to avoid as many personal triggers as possible to prevent reaching your migraine threshold.

Unfortunately, it is not as simple as staying away from common triggers and thereby never experiencing a migraine again. The disorder is far more complicated than that, but purposely avoiding triggers can certainly decrease the number of migraines you experience. Use the migraine diary in chapter 1 to identify any common precursors to your migraines. Perhaps you always suffer from migraines after a long drive in a hot car, after sleeping in on Sundays, or after eating a particular food.

Some triggers, such as bright sunlight or a stressful new job, are unavoidable and will have to be dealt with as they arise. Other triggers, however, are very much controllable. Triggering foods and drinks will be discussed in part 2 of this book; for now, we will focus on controllable environmental factors.

Computers

Most people cannot avoid using computers, but there are things you can do to reduce your risk of an associated attack. Always sit with good posture, and take regular breaks to stand up and move away from your screen. Use anti-glare screens, and work in a room filled with natural light where possible. Standing desks are another option you may wish to look into.

Estrogen

As mentioned, the effect of hormonal contraception and other medications containing estrogen varies on a case-by-case basis. If you fear your medication is worsening your migraines, try seeking an alternative. In addition, always inform your doctor that you suffer from migraines before taking any such medication.

Light, Smells, and Noise

If you have a hard time with bright lights, wear sunglasses and a hat where possible. Your employer is legally obliged to change the lighting if it interferes with your personal comfort, so there is no need to suffer beneath fluorescent lights all day long. Similarly, if one of your colleagues is wearing an overpowering amount of perfume or cologne, the law is in your favor. If you find yourself in a loud environment and cannot do much about it, try wearing earplugs or listening to calming music.

Sleep

Aim for seven to eight hours of sleep each night, and always try to go to bed and wake up at the same time every day. As tempting as it can be to sleep in on weekends, remember that too much sleep can also trigger migraines.

Stress Levels

Actively attempt to reduce your stress levels. Avoid stressful situations where possible, and limit the amount of overtime you perform at work. Incorporate techniques such as meditation and yoga into your life, and try simple relaxation methods such as listening to music, reading, or unwinding in a hot bath.

Get Physical

Although some people can barely move when they are struck with a migraine, some find that gentle exercise in the prodrome or aura phase can help delay or even prevent a migraine from progressing further. Sudden, intense exercise such as weight lifting or sprinting can provoke or exacerbate headaches, so they may be best avoided.

Aerobic Exercise

Regular aerobic exercise can reduce tension and help prevent migraines. As well as having a therapeutic effect, cardiovascular exercise has the added bonus of relieving stress and improving quality of sleep, which are two major migraine triggers in themselves. Exercise stimulates the release of pain-relieving chemicals known as endorphins, as well as the natural antidepressants enkephalins.

Safe forms of aerobic exercise include walking, jogging, swimming, dancing, and cycling. It is important to thoroughly warm-up when taking part in these activities to avoid placing sudden and unexpected demands on your body for oxygen, which will often trigger a migraine. You should

SEX & ORGASM HEADACHES

How many of us have heard the line, "Not tonight, honey; I have a headache"? While sex can indeed intensify the pain of a migraine or even trigger an attack, in some cases it can help relieve the pain. The effect of sex and its accompanying orgasm depends on the person and the circumstances.

Some believe that sex can cause a headache due to the increase in blood pressure and dilation of the blood vessels within the brain. Others believe that sex, particularly when it ends with an orgasm, releases certain chemicals including serotonin, which help alleviate a migraine. Sex also releases endorphins, which are natural instant painkillers. If you do find that having an orgasm relieves your migraine pain but you do not have access to a willing partner, self-pleasure will do the trick just as well!

Physical activity can trigger migraines in some individuals, and sex counts as an active pursuit. The act itself puts pressure on the back and neck, which can provoke a migraine. Usually, sex-related migraines are unpredictable and do not occur every time. Although women are more prone to suffer from migraines in general, according to Migraine.com, men are four times more likely to develop a migraine during sex.

The most common type of headache triggered by sex is known as an *explosive headache*. Occurring at the point of orgasm, it has similar symptoms to those of a brain hemorrhage. You should seek immediate medical attention the first time you experience such a headache to indeed rule out the possibility that something more serious has occurred.

also ensure that you are well hydrated and have eaten a substantial meal before exercising.

Try exercising for at least 30 minutes, 5 times per week. Evaluate any improvements in your migraines after six weeks.

Stretching

While yoga is great for improving overall health and well-being, you may not have the time to commit to regular classes. You may also not have any interest in performing stretches other than those that have been specifically linked to migraine improvement.

Many people experience great benefits from spending just five to ten minutes per day stretching, particularly focusing on the neck, shoulders, and back muscles. Tightness in these muscles due to either stress or poor posture often causes migraines. Furthermore, when you have a migraine, your muscles usually tense even more as you naturally try to avoid moving your head. If you suffer from frequent attacks, the muscles in your neck and shoulders may therefore become shortened, chronically fatigued, and irritated. My massage therapist commented that my neck and shoulders were the tightest they have ever been during my most frequent bout of migraines.

Stretching daily will help reverse these effects. You should perform shoulder and head rolls, slowly look from side to side, and twist your upper torso in both directions.

Yoga

As previously mentioned, yoga is a great tool for managing stress. Yoga is an ancient exercise technique that promotes holistic living through a combination of postures and breathing techniques. It helps relieve stress and tension in the body and improves circulation. Unlike aerobic exercise, yoga is extremely low impact and unlikely to trigger a migraine attack.

Forward-folding postures such as child's pose and downward dog are particularly helpful for migraineurs, as they increase blood supply to the brain. Yoga teaches you how to breathe slowly and deeply, which is also effective as a relaxation tool.

Yoga does not require any equipment, and it can be learned either in classes or at home using books and tapes. Avoid any classes that take place in a heated room, and instead try a basic vinyasa or hatha class.

Many migraineurs report an improvement in their condition from taking just one yoga class per week.

Natural Remedies

Nontraditional therapies such as acupuncture, aromatherapy, biofeedback, cognitive behavioral therapy, and massage therapy are often reported to bring about more improvements in migraineurs' conditions than standard medication. Many also prefer to use a more natural means of treatment rather than having to rely upon artificial chemicals and the negative side effects they often entail. Most natural treatment options have very few—if any—associated risks.

It is rare that only one of these natural remedies will work to make a difference in the frequency or severity of your migraine attacks, so it is best to use a combination of methods while also paying attention to your triggers.

Acupuncture

When considering alternative methods of treatment, the best place to start may involve moving away from traditional Western medicine completely and instead looking at the Chinese practice of acupuncture. *Acupuncture* involves the insertion of tiny needles into specific points on the surface of your body, which is then followed by gentle manual or electrical stimulation. The needles are typically left in the body for 20 to 30 minutes. This causes blood vessels in the area to dilate, thereby enhancing blood flow. Acupuncture also relaxes the nervous system around the central pain pathways and prompts the release of endorphins. Both of these effects are thought to elicit a healing response in migraineurs.

Acupuncture has been used to treat migraines and tension headaches for thousands of years. The practice has almost no side effects.

Aromatherapy

Aromatherapy involves the use of essential oils extracted from plants to relieve the pain of headaches. The practice can be administered by a qualified aromatherapist or conducted yourself in the privacy of your own home. Certain scents are believed to be especially effective against migraines, such as bergamot, chamomile, eucalyptus, lavender, peppermint, rosemary, and sandalwood. They can either be inhaled or dropped on to the head or neck in the form of an oil.

There is not much scientific research to back up the practice of aromatherapy. However, it is extremely safe and has been used to successfully treat both physiological and psychological ailments for thousands of years.

Although aromatherapy cannot cure a migraine, it can provide symptomatic relief, particularly from nausea. Aside from the smells themselves being therapeutic, essential oils can also directly affect the body's chemistry and alter the body's pain perception.

For those who are extremely sensitive to smells during a migraine attack, aromatherapy may not work; however, many who are sensitive report no problems with most essential oils. Furthermore, some report that if they are exposed to a triggering smell but get a hold of their preferred essential oil fast enough, they can prevent a migraine from developing. You may see a positive response in only a few minutes.

For some, applying pressure can help relieve pain. In the midst of an attack, lie down in a dark, quiet room with a cold, wet cloth on your forehead or the back of your neck. Press your thumbs firmly into the bridge of your nose, just beneath your forehead. Then place one thumb on each eyebrow, and apply pressure upward toward your forehead. Finally, take your thumbs or three middle fingers and press them firmly into your temples, adding a small circular motion. Hold each of these pressure points for 10 seconds, and repeat as necessary.

Biofeedback

Biofeedback involves the use of small metal sensors that measure the shifts in your heart rate, skin temperature, muscle tension, and brain waves in response to physical changes. This provides feedback about how the body responds to pain, which you can then attempt to control by learning stress-reduction skills.

Biofeedback is often referred to as a "mind over migraine" treatment tool, as it aims to teach you how to relax and control your physical state through your thoughts. The goal is to learn how to influence the blood flow to your brain and better manage your episodes. With practice, you will be able to implement the same techniques without the help of any special equipment.

This type of therapy is most effective in preventing migraines before they occur, although many do report that employing the same techniques during an attack can lessen its severity and duration.

When it comes to reducing the frequency and length of migraine episodes, many studies claim that the effects of biofeedback are on par with those of many traditional Western drugs but, importantly, are not accompanied by any of their negative side effects. The one downside to biofeedback is that it requires time and financial commitments as well as a moderate amount of effort from the patient. Sessions typically last 30 to 60 minutes, and you may need anywhere between 10 and 50 sessions to learn how to properly control your physical responses.

Chiropractic Therapy

Chiropractic therapy involves the manipulation, movement, and stretching of the spine. By analyzing a migraineur's spinal health, chiropractors use their hands as well as devices such as straps and braces to reduce the frequency of migraines. Chiropractic treatment is thought to have the added benefit of stress relief, which also assists in preventing migraines. Chiropractors will also provide information about correct posture and specific exercises that can relieve spinal tension.

This is a preventative measure, and will not help a migraineur if already in the throes of an attack. Research confirming its efficiency as a treatment method is still to be determined, but it is believed to be most effective in migraineurs that experience neck pain either before or during an episode. Unlike most of the other natural treatment methods, chiropractic therapy has a few negative side effects, including discomfort during treatment, increased pain and stiffness, and often an initial increase in headaches after treatment has begun.

Cognitive Behavioral Therapy

Cognitive behavioral therapy, otherwise known as "talk therapy," is based on the link between mind and body. It involves working with a psychologist to change your thoughts and behaviors to help reduce your frequency of migraines.

Treatment may involve incorporating relaxation and stress management strategies, managing migraine triggers, participating in more activities to increase wellness, and modifying your thoughts to make them more favorable to your condition.

This type of therapy is most beneficial for those who have difficulty managing their triggers, particularly stress. The therapy is not so much about avoiding stress as it is about handling that stress. In theory, by controlling your mind you should be able to control your body.

Massage Therapy

Massage improves relaxation and relieves muscle tension. Massage may be self-administered or provided by a professional or friend. The scientific evidence proving the effectiveness of massage is limited, but many migraineurs report an improvement in their condition, particularly when they combine this remedy with other treatment options.

This type of therapy does not typically stop migraines once they have started. Although massages can provide temporary relief, some people report experiencing some of their most intense head pain following a massage. It is instead better used as a preventive technique to ease stress and reduce future incidence of migraines.

Various types of massage that can be beneficial for migraineurs:

- *Craniosacral therapy* involves massaging the skull and scalp, which soothes your nerves and lessens pain waves.
- *Neuromuscular massage,* or trigger-point therapy, applies pressure to specific points in the body to reduce nerve compression and relieve tension.

- *Acupressure* involves applying gentle finger pressure to various points on the head.
- *Reflexology* is based on massaging specific points on the soles of the feet that are closely linked to relieving stress and pain in migraineurs who suffer from headaches.
- *Deep tissue massage* uses pressure, movement, and stretching to improve circulation and reduce muscle tension, particularly in the shoulders and neck.

You can combine massage therapy with aromatherapy by using lavender or peppermint massage oil.

Physiotherapy

Physiotherapy, or physical therapy, is particularly beneficial for migraineurs who suffer neck pain. Physiotherapy works to treat dysfunction in the musculoskeletal tissues of the upper cervical spine, by increasing the range of motion in the neck and restoring neutral posture. Treatment may be administered via manual therapy, postural and movement reeducation, and ergonomic correction. It can be used as a preventive method before the onset of a migraine as well as during the initial throes of an attack.

Physiotherapy has no negative side effects, other than the headache that often appears during the initial treatment—but this is necessary to determine if a migraine is indeed caused by a spine dysfunction.

Vitamins and Supplements

The following supplements are most commonly believed to ease migraine symptoms and pain. Many of these herbal remedies have been used for thousands of years. Before you start taking a supplement, speak with your doctor to ensure it will not cause a negative reaction with any other medications you are taking or conditions you have.

SUPPLEMENT	PROPERTIES	HOW IT CAN HELP
COENZYME Q10	Creates adenosine triphosphate in the body, which serves as a major energy source within cells and also acts as an antioxidant.	Coenzyme Q10 is a well-known treatment for mitochondrial disorders. Some research has shown that low brain energy plays a role in developing migraines, and coenzyme Q10 counteracts that by serving as a vital cofactor to the enzymes responsible for the production of adenosine triphosphate (Life Enhancement, 2005). Recommended dosage for migraineurs is 100mg three times per day.
FEVERFEW (TANACETUM PARTHENIUM)	Anti-inflammatory (reduces inflammation), antipyretic (prevents fever), antispasmodic (relieves muscle spasms), and cardiotonic (increases the heart's force of contraction).	Blocks the chemicals in the body that cause inflammation and are responsible for blood vessel dilation and constriction, both of which lead to migraines (Migraine.com, 2010). Helps ease the pain, nausea, and sensitivity to light that occur during a migraine and reduces the number of attacks (WebMD, 2009). Recommended dosage for migraineurs is 50 to 100mg daily.
MAGNESIUM	Vital to multiple physiological processes, including calcium absorption and blood pressure regulation. Also acts as a muscle relaxant.	Migraineurs often have low levels of magnesium in the brain. As this mineral is necessary for the proper performance of serotonin, there may be a connection between migraines and magnesium deficiency. In addition, those with low magnesium levels often find that their arteries constrict more. Magnesium can also help relieve tension in the neck and shoulders (Magnesium Online Resource Center, 2008). Supplementation is particularly helpful for women who suffer from menstrual-related migraines. Recommended dosage for migraineurs varies between 200 and 600mg per day.
RIBOFLAVIN (VITAMIN B2)	Converts food to energy and works as an antioxidant by removing free radicals.	Reduces migraine frequency and duration due to the positive effect it has on oxygen metabolism within the brain (The Migraine Trust, 2007). Usual dose for migraineurs is 400mg daily.

N ow that you know what a migraine is, and have an understanding of how it occurs, it is time to be proactive in your treatment approach. After reading part 1, you should understand how to avoid many common environmental triggers. It is now time to turn your focus toward your diet.

The second part of this book demonstrates how to modify your diet to reduce your risk of suffering migraines by explaining exactly what you should and should not be eating and why. It is important to have a thorough understanding of the theory behind any diet before you attempt to follow it.

We will then guide you through the elimination phase, providing clear instructions and meal plans for both the 3-day cleanse and the 28-day meal plan. This section is filled with a number of helpful tips to ensure the process is as easy as possible, and it will give you an idea of what to expect during this period. Finally, we will explain how to commence the reintroduction phase to determine exactly which triggers are problematic for you. Once you have finished reading this section, you will possess the knowledge required to take control of your diet for the rest of your life in order to minimize your migraine episodes.

PART

2

PLAN OF ATTACK

Chapter Three

A Dietary Approach

For many years it has been thought that diet has a close and intricate relationship with the onset of migraines. In a 2005 food intolerance study, researchers found that 30 to 40 percent of migraineurs who eliminated certain foods from their diet reported an improvement in their condition. Furthermore, more than 60 percent claimed that their migraine symptoms returned when they reincorporated those foods back into their diet (Rees et al., 2005).

Although a significant amount of anecdotal evidence supports the connection between diet and migraines, the scientific research confirming the link is still in its early stages. In addition, the lack of scientific understanding as to how migraines actually occur makes it difficult to pinpoint exactly why several foods such as processed meats, dairy, refined and artificial sugars, caffeine, and alcohol seem to trigger negative reactions among migraineurs.

It is important to remember that theories in this area are still evolving, and it is difficult to recommend a single diet that will work for everyone. That said, there are clear benefits involved in eliminating certain triggers, but it will require patience and persistence on behalf of the individual wishing to use diet as a means of treatment.

Many people overlook the important role diet plays in their health, instead focusing on traditional medicine and, occasionally, alternative health treatments. However, it makes sense that what you place inside your body will be reflected on the outside. If you eat junk food day in and day out, you should not be surprised to feel lethargic and unfit. On the other hand, if you eat more natural and nutritious foods, you will likely feel more energetic and healthier overall.

The Ideal Diet

The ideal diet to prevent migraines is wholesome, natural, and unprocessed. This diet contains no processed food or sugar, it has its foundation in fresh fruits and vegetables, it is free of common allergenic foods such as gluten, soy, and dairy, and it contains limited amounts of caffeine and alcohol. It will take you back to a style of eating that is more natural for all bodies to process and digest.

The medicinal properties of food have been harnessed for thousands of years. Recently, you may have heard about the Paleo diet, which is based on what our early ancestors ate. This diet has surged in popularity as it is not only believed to treat a number of ailments but also reportedly has its followers looking and feeling better than ever. The diet prescribed in this book is similar to the Paleo diet in that it avoids dairy and most grains and legumes.

Migraineurs are not the only ones who can benefit from following a diet such as this. Human bodies are best suited to this type of diet because it is high in nutrients, it improves digestive health, and it stabilizes blood sugar levels. This diet is anti-inflammatory, which, as we know from discussing the alternative treatment methods in chapter 2, is crucial to preventing migraines.

Finally, if you are currently overweight, it may help with weight loss. For those already within a healthy weight range, following this diet will help you maintain that. This is especially important considering that obesity is commonly thought to be a factor in the development of migraines.

Low/No Sugar

Due to the prevalence of sugar in Western diets, it is almost impossible to avoid it completely. However, you can take steps to limit how much you consume.

Sugar is found in the usual culprits such as pastries, sodas, and desserts, but it is also in less obvious foods such as pasta, rice, cereals, granola bars, fruit juice, yogurt, spaghetti sauce, chips, pretzels, mayonnaise, and ketchup. Study food labels, and avoid any product listing brown sugar, cane sugar, corn syrup, fruit juice concentrate, high-fructose corn syrup, honey, maple syrup, molasses, or sugar molecules ending in "ose" (e.g., dextrose, fructose, glucose, lactose, maltose, or sucrose) in its ingredients. Even better, do not consume anything that has an ingredients list.

Sugar is considered to be a common migraine trigger due to its effect on blood sugar levels. The aforementioned foods are high on the glycemic index and cause glucose levels to rise and then fall rapidly as your body releases insulin. This plummet also causes blood pressure to rise. These concurrent events may cause migraines. Because of the crash in blood sugar levels, many people—including myself—crave bland carbohydrates such as bread, mashed potatoes, and pasta in the midst of a migraine attack.

Cutting out sugar will have a dramatic impact on your overall health. It will often result in weight loss, an improved immune system, and a decreased risk of heart disease and diabetes. Sugar has no nutritional properties and simply adds unnecessary calories to your diet.

Use natural alternatives such as fruit, cinnamon, and vanilla to sweeten your foods instead. Stevia, a natural sweetener that comes from the stevia plant, is preferable to other natural, yet sugar-laden, sweeteners such as agave, honey, and maple syrup.

Low/No Dairy

You should avoid all types of dairy, including skim or whole cow's milk, goat's milk, butter, cheese, cream, custard, ice cream, and yogurt. As with sugar, cutting back on dairy will provide a host of benefits other than reducing the frequency of your migraines. This is because the majority of people—around 75 percent, according to Collective Evolution (2013)—are lactose intolerant, and migraines are the body's way of rejecting lactose.

The increased rate of diseases and allergies in society in recent years corresponds with the surge in processed foods, including grains and dairy. The problem is not typically the foods themselves but rather the way they are produced; during production, most of the nutrients are stripped away as unnecessary sugar and chemicals are added.

Humans are the only animals that drink milk beyond infancy and the only species to consume the milk of another animal. As mentioned, around 75 percent of people cannot digest dairy properly due to the lactose it contains, meaning they may experience bloating, diarrhea, nausea, or even vomiting (Pribila et al., 2000). This is because dairy products are created through a destructive pasteurization process, which kills germs but also destroys beneficial nutrients, including those that make digestion possible. Furthermore, cows are pumped full of hormones to make them grow bigger and produce more milk, and they are also often given low-quality foods, which translates to hormonal problems and sinus congestion in humans.

Many people worry that eliminating dairy products will lead to a calcium deficiency. The idea that milk consumption is necessary for strong bones is largely the result of marketing ploys. Consider that Japanese people consume limited amounts of dairy and yet maintain lower rates of osteoporosis and higher life expectancies than those in the United States (Fallon and Enig, 2000). There are other sources of calcium that are not problematic to a migraineur such as broccoli, cabbage, kale, spinach, eggs, fish, and berries.

Aside from dairy milk and its common alternative, soy, there are plenty of other options available including unsweetened almond, coconut, and rice milk.

Limited Caffeine

Caffeine may be either beneficial or harmful for a migraineur, but we will err on the side of caution and assume that it is a trigger. The problem is not typically with caffeine itself but with the fact you can easily become physically dependent on it. When you are used to regularly consuming caffeine and you suddenly do not, the blood vessels within your brain will dilate—often resulting in a migraine. This can occur simply from sleeping in and missing your regular cup of morning coffee. Hence, it is better to completely eliminate caffeine from your life to avoid experiencing caffeine withdrawal during these unavoidable situations.

You should always avoid having more than two servings, or 200mg total, of caffeine per day. However, for the purposes of the elimination diet, you will cut it out altogether. Remember that caffeine is not only found in the most obvious suspects such as coffee, tea, and cola but also in chocolate and over-the-counter painkillers. Water and decaffeinated herbal teas are the ideal beverages of choice during the elimination phase.

Limited Alcohol

Alcohol in general is problematic for migraineurs. Firstly, drinking increases blood flow to your brain, which can in turn cause blood vessel dilation. Secondly, some scientists believe the byproducts of alcohol metabolization cause migraines. Lastly, alcohol has a dehydrating effect, which can make you more susceptible to an attack.

The most problematic types of alcohol are beer, red wine, sparkling wine, and whiskey. Only the smallest amounts of alcohol are needed to trigger a migraine in those who are vulnerable, so it is best to abstain completely.

Gluten-Free

Gluten refers to the proteins found in wheat, rye, barley, and triticale. It helps foods maintain their shape and functions as a glue that holds certain food together. Gluten-free diets have surged in popularity in recent years, even among those who do not have celiac disease—a disease whereby the consumption of gluten leads to inflammation of the small intestine and, subsequently, one's ability to absorb nutrients is compromised.

Studies and personal testimonials have shown that the brains and digestive systems of many people function best when following a gluten-free diet, with as many as 18 million Americans believed to be gluten sensitive (Celiac Central, 2015). This sensitivity typically manifests itself in digestive problems, such as bloating, constipation, or diarrhea.

What is most problematic for migraineurs, however, is gluten's effect on the brain. Research has shown that, following the initial response in your digestive tract after consuming gluten, your nervous system becomes oversensitive and inflamed (Cady et al., 2012). In turn, this negatively affects the body's immune response and ability to absorb nutrients.

Humans have only been consuming grains for less than 1 percent of their existence, so it is no surprise that many people's bodies have not adapted. As with dairy, the production process for foods containing gluten has evolved for the worse. Only 50 years ago, bread was baked via a long process featuring a slow fermentation of the dough. This has been sped up to less than three hours, and yeast levels have been increased to deal with the reduced fermenting period, meaning that gluten and starches are no longer given sufficient time to convert to a digestible form.

Furthermore, gluten itself contains tightly bonded amino acids that are highly resistant to human digestion. Most people consume far too many grains, leading to constantly inflamed and damaged intestinal linings.

Implementing a gluten-free diet does not give you free rein to gorge yourself on all the gluten-free cakes and breads, however. These foods can be problematic for migraineurs due to their sugar and additives and are therefore best avoided. Instead, replace products containing gluten with fruits, vegetables, and alternative sources of starchy carbohydrates such as sweet potatoes, rice, and quinoa.

An Abundance of Fruits and Vegetables

After discussing what you should limit or avoid altogether, you may be wondering what is left. The good news is there is still plenty of food available that will suit your new dietary requirements.

The base of your diet should consist of a wide range of fresh fruits and vegetables, excluding those listed as triggers in the following section. Fruits and vegetables contain a large number of nutrients—including fiber, folate, potassium, and vitamins A, C, and E—and have very few aggravating properties for migraineurs. They also have a high water content, which helps with staying hydrated and keeping migraines at bay.

Fruits and vegetables can be especially beneficial for helping women avoid migraines. This is because all fruits and vegetables contain plant estrogens that blunt the negative effects of the natural estrogen within our bodies, which is particularly helpful for those who suffer menstrual-related migraines.

Although fruit is high in sugar, it contains other desirable nutrients and does not need to be removed from the diet. While it is important to avoid fruit juice and dried fruit—which contain added sugar—you may have two to three servings of fresh fruit per day. The best choices for migraineurs are berries, cherries, pears, and prunes. However, note that during the initial 3-day cleanse you will avoid fruit in order to limit your sugar intake.

High in Protein

Consume high-protein foods such as seafood, meat, and poultry, as well as vegetarian options such as eggs, legumes, seeds, and nondairy yogurts. Protein is important for regular body functioning as well as increasing satiety levels.

Seafood products are high in protein and contain a number of important nutrients, such as vitamin D and omega-3 fatty acids. Fatty types of fish such as mackerel, salmon, trout, and tuna contain the most nutrients that are essential for a healthy mind and body.

Meat, poultry, and eggs are more great sources of protein and healthy fats. They contain essential nutrients, such as vitamin B_{12} and iron. If it fits your budget, try to purchase grass-fed and organic meat products.

Chia, flax, hemp, pumpkin, and sunflower seeds are not only high in protein but also high in monounsaturated fats. Consuming sufficient amounts of healthy fats is essential for optimal heart health, proper brain function, and weight maintenance. Many of these seeds are also high in calcium, iron, fiber, folate, and magnesium—the latter of which was recommended as a supplement for migraineurs in chapter 2.

Triggering Foods

This section looks at some common dietary triggers in detail and explores why they are believed to cause a negative reaction for migraineurs. There is still much to be learned regarding how each of these foods actually elicits a negative response, but the following foods seem to commonly act as triggers for migraineurs.

Alcohol

Red wine and beer are the worst culprits when it comes to triggering migraine attacks, as they both contain tyramine. Many also report adverse reactions to champagne and whiskey.

Artificial Sweeteners

Some people may think they can replace the sugar they will be eliminating from their diets with artificial sweeteners. Sadly, they are mistaken. Not only do sweeteners contain negative properties that can trigger migraines, but they also increase your desire for sweet foods and thus make it more difficult to stop eating sugar.

Although sweeteners such as acesulfame, aspartame, saccharin, and sucralose do not contain sugar and therefore do not increase blood sugar levels after consumption, they still elicit the release of insulin.

Aspartame is the most common sweetener, and it is found in more than 6,000 products globally. Avoid consuming sweeteners in the form of diet beverages, light yogurts, sugar-free candies, and low-calorie desserts, and instead

66 My migraines always start with a brief loss of peripheral vision, then everything in my line of sight narrows to a pinpoint. I don't experience pain, but I do experience visual disturbances—like prolonged auras—that lead to vertigo and nausea. Occasionally I'll experience numbness in my extremities. Even without the pain, I'm still unable to fully function for a few hours. I started getting migraines in my teens and struggled with them throughout my twenties. Now I'm careful about what I eat, avoid alcohol as much as possible, and keep myself hydrated. 99

—Ethan, age 42, California

turn to the natural sweeteners stevia, cinnamon, and vanilla. By giving up artificial sweeteners, you will gain the same benefits as you will by cutting back on your sugar intake, including weight loss and a reduced risk of type 2 diabetes.

Certain Fruits

Certain fruits contain tyramine and are best avoided. They include plums, cranberries, bananas, avocados, tangerines, pineapple, citrus, and dried fruits. Citrus fruits and bananas contain both tyramine and histamine, both of which widen blood vessels. Red-skinned apples and pears contain tannins, which appear to be a trigger for many.

Certain Vegetables

Vegetables that have been shown to trigger migraines include beets, eggplants, chili peppers, string beans, garlic, and onion, as they contain either nitrates or tyramine.

A special note should be made about corn. Corn is present in a number of common foods in the standard Western diet. Over the years, corn has become increasingly subject to genetic modification. This has increased its production rate and resistance to pests but has also increased its likelihood of causing weight gain and disease (Samsel, 2012). Depending on its eventual form, it may no longer be classified as a vegetable but rather a grain. Corn contains small amounts of nitrates, but its most harmful form for migraineurs is corn syrup.

While you should aim to fill your plate with a broad range of fruits and vegetables, it is wise to steer clear of the preceding types until you are sure they are not triggers for you. In addition, purchasing organic vegetables may further reduce your exposure to nitrates, according to EatRight Ontario.

Dairy

All dairy products contain a protein called casein, and it is this protein that makes dairy problematic for migraineurs. Headaches result when one has even mild lactose intolerance—and, unfortunately, most of us do. Cultured dairy products such as yogurt, sour cream, and buttermilk are among the worst offenders. Low-fat and skim milk products are also particularly troublesome as they are often loaded with sugar to make up for the lack of flavor from fat.

Foods Containing Tyramine

Tyramine is a compound produced by the breakdown of the amino acid tyrosine, which causes blood vessel dilation. For those who take monoamine oxidase (MAO) inhibitor medications to treat their migraines, it is extremely important to avoid all foods containing tyramine, as these foods can lead to severely high blood pressure.

Tyramine is found naturally in foods such as nuts, soy (which is found in many Asian sauces, bean sprouts, edamame, tempeh, and tofu), yogurt, fava beans, sausages, and citrus fruits, as well as in aged or fermented foods such as cheese (particularly blue, Cheddar, Gouda, Parmesan, and Swiss), sauerkraut, sourdough bread, pickled livers, and smoked fish. Generally, the longer a high-protein food ages, the greater its tyramine content becomes.

To minimize your exposure to tyramine, eat fresh produce within two days of purchase, do not eat spoiled foods, thaw food in the refrigerator rather than at room temperature, and eat canned or frozen foods immediately after opening.

Monosodium Glutamate (MSG)

Monosodium glutamate (MSG) is possibly the best-known food additive. It is used as a food preservative and flavor enhancer. It has a poor reputation for causing migraines but also cramping, diarrhea, sweating, and chest pain. Not only is the glutamate in MSG a blood vessel dilator, it is also an excitatory neurotransmitter, which increases activity in certain areas of the brain and is therefore closely linked to migraines.

MSG is found in many Asian dishes as well as Parmesan cheese, canned meats, stocks and soups, and almost every product that contains soy proteins.

Salty/Processed Foods

Many processed foods contain gluten, sugar, or MSG—all of which can be problematic for migraineurs. Processed meats such as bacon, ham, salami, and sausages contain nitrates, which increase the production of nitric oxide—a gas that expands blood vessels. They are added to food for added flavor as well as their preservative qualities.

Chapter Four

3-Day Cleanse and 28-Day Meal Plan

A s you can see, the list of possible migraine-triggering foods is extensive and can be overwhelming. You may feel confused and unsure where to start. You may wonder how you can safely eliminate so many foods without causing any detriment to your health. The good news is that the following pages will take all the guesswork out for you. You'll start with a 3-day cleanse and continue with a 28-day meal plan. Then, you'll be ready to move on to shopping lists and meal plans to make the transition as smooth as possible. In part 3, you will find all the delicious, simple-to-prepare recipes featured in the meal plans.

The recipes adhere to a more traditional style of eating, with plenty of fresh fruits and vegetables, and include a number of healthy, nutritious, and anti-inflammatory foods. Protein-rich foods such as lean poultry, eggs, oats, and rice will boost serotonin levels, which can help prevent migraines.

Due to the aforementioned importance of maintaining stable blood sugar levels, you should aim to eat three meals plus two to three snacks per day. Each meal should be made up of a combination of protein, healthy fats, and low-glycemic carbs. Many people make the mistake of eating snacks composed of carbohydrates only, such as fruit, which leads to spikes in blood sugar levels. Instead, always consume fruit with a protein and fat source, such as coconut milk yogurt with a handful of berries and nuts. In conjunction, you may see benefits in supplementing your diet with some of the vitamins discussed in chapter 2.

Eliminating all possible triggers for a specific period of time is crucial so your body can completely remove all of these foods from your system. Chapter 5 tells you how to start adding some of the potential triggers back into your diet, one at a time, to determine exactly which foods cause you problems. You can use this new information to either permanently avoid your strongest triggers, or avoid them at times when you are at a high risk of suffering from an attack. For example, a woman may only experience migraines when she has her period, so there is no need for her to avoid her trigger foods at other times of the month.

Because triggers are individualized, the only way to determine what applies to you is by doing a thorough and comprehensive elimination diet, as outlined in this chapter. Although the elimination process may be painful and frustrating at first, discovering the true triggers of your migraines will be worth it in the long run.

If you are pregnant or breastfeeding, an elimination diet may not be appropriate. It is best to discuss any planned dietary changes with your doctor.

Keeping Track

As you progress through the elimination phase, it is important to keep track of how your body reacts. Do not start when you are in the middle of a pain cycle; rather, wait until you are relatively pain-free, and eliminate all of the previously mentioned triggers.

Make a note of how you feel each day. You can then use these notes, in conjunction with your migraine diary from chapter 1, to monitor any changes in your attacks. As explained later in this chapter, the changes may not always be initially positive; however, it is important to fight through any temporary discomfort to reap the benefits.

You may find yourself feeling better following this type of diet, regardless of whether it positively affects your migraines. In addition, the act of following a specific diet has been shown to produce therapeutic effects—similarly to the cognitive behavioral therapy discussed in chapter 2—as you will feel more in control of your migraines. That said, you should not be too strict if you do not have to be; if you insist on eliminating all possible triggers for an extended period of time, you will likely only create more stress within your body.

STOCKING YOUR PANTRY AND TOOLBOX

You will begin by removing all trigger foods from your pantry so that there is no temptation to stray from the plan. In any case, only a limited amount of food will enter your pantry, as most of the foods on this plan are fresh and will need to be stored in the fridge. Foods to stock in your pantry include a variety of dried herbs and spices, nondairy boxed milks, rice, coconut oil, stevia, and vanilla extract.

Almost any herb or spice is suitable for migraineurs, including allspice, basil, bay leaves, black pepper, cardamom, cinnamon, coriander, cumin, curry powder, dill, fennel seed, mint, nutmeg, oregano, paprika, rosemary, saffron, sage, sea salt, and thyme. Ginger is thought to be especially beneficial for migraineurs. According to Migraine.com, it helps ease nausea and is also believed to block prostaglandins, the hormones that cause inflammation of the blood vessels in the brain. About one quarter of a teaspoon of fresh powdered ginger is recommended at the onset of a migraine.

In terms of useful kitchen gadgets to invest in, a food processor and a slow cooker will save you a great deal of time and effort when cooking. You can prepare a number of healthy meals in bulk with minimal effort using a slow cooker, and a food processor will cut down on time spent chopping and mixing.

You will also need at least one frying pan and one pot to cook your meals in, as well as a chopping board and a good-quality chef's knife for preparing the meat and vegetables on the plan.

About the 3-Day Cleanse

You will begin your elimination diet with a 3-day cleanse. During this time, you will eliminate all of the foods previously flagged as triggers. This phase of the plan will be the most difficult, but it will also help you build momentum, and you may feel significantly better by the end of the cleanse. Make sure you are well organized before you start the cleanse, using the shopping and pantry lists within this chapter to stock up on the essentials.

It is imperative to follow the cleanse as outlined, as well as the following 28-day plan. Do not skip meals or snacks or stray from the list of approved foods. In chapter 5, you will learn how to reincorporate some of the foods you have eliminated and thereby customize the diet to suit your personal triggers and preferences. This chart is also available for download at callistomedia.com /migrainereliefdiet.

Symptom Tracker / 3-Day Cleanse

		DAY 1	DAY 2	DAY 3
MORNING	Foods			
	Symptoms			
AFTERNOON	Foods			
	Symptoms			
EVENING	Foods			
	Symptoms			

3-Day Cleanse Meal Plan

The recipes for the 3-day cleanse can be found in part 3 of this book. Remember to follow the meal plan exactly, adding in two snacks per day from the approved snack list. It is best to start this cleanse on a Friday so you can commence week one of the 28-day plan on a Monday. This will also give you plenty of time on the weekend to prepare yourself for the longer plan.

FRIDAY

Breakfast: Simple Turkey Sausage (page 103)

Lunch: Ginger–Chicken Wraps (page 130)

Dinner: Baked Tilapia with Bok Choy and Spinach (page 126)

SATURDAY

Breakfast: Chicken and Pumpkin Hash (page 102)

Lunch: Shaved Brussels Sprout and Herb Salad (page 106)

Dinner: Butternut Squash and Chickpea Bowl (page 153)

SUNDAY

Breakfast: Celeriac and Sweet Potato Pancakes (page 98)

Lunch: Grilled Lamb Chops with Mint Pesto (page 136)

Dinner: Chicken–Broccoli Casserole (page 133)

Suggested Snacks

Celery, cucumber, and carrot sticks

Gluten-free crackers

4 slices deli roast beef (gluten-free)

4 gluten-free tortillas with hummus

8 ounces coconut milk yogurt

2 hardboiled eggs

SHOPPING LIST

FRUITS AND VEGETABLES

Bok choy (2 cups chopped)

Broccoli (1 head)

Brussels sprouts (2 pounds)

Butternut squash (1)

Carrots (5)

Celeriac root (2)

Celery stalk (1)

English cucumbers (2)

Fennel bulb (1)

Jicama (1)

Kale (2 cups)

Lettuce, Boston (1 head)

Pumpkin (2 pounds)

Red bell peppers (2)

Scallions (7)

Shallots (2)

Spinach (2 cups)

Sweet potatoes (2)

DAIRY, DAIRY ALTERNATIVES, AND EGGS

Coconut milk yogurt, plain (8 ounces)

Cream cheese (1 cup)

Eggs (½ dozen)

Rice milk, unsweetened (1 cup)

FRESH HERBS AND SPICES

Basil (1 bunch)

Cilantro (1 bunch)

Ginger (1 knob)

Parsley (1 bunch)

Thyme (1 bunch)

FISH AND SEAFOOD

Tilapia fillets (4, 8-ounce)

MEAT AND POULTRY

Chicken breast, boneless, skinless (3½ pounds)

Ground turkey (1 pound)

Lamb, loin chops, about one inch thick (8)

Roast beef, deli-sliced, gluten-free (8 ounces)

PANTRY ITEMS

Arrowroot powder

Black pepper, freshly ground

Chickpeas, canned

Cinnamon, ground

Cloves, ground

Cumin, ground

Mustard, grainy

Nonstick olive oil cooking spray

Nutmeg, ground

Oil, coconut

Red pepper flakes

Sea salt

White vinegar

OTHER

Chickpeas, canned (2 cups)

Gluten-free crackers (1 pack)

Gluten-free tortillas (4)

Hummus (1 pack)

Stevia (1, 7g) packet

White rice (3 cups)

28-Day Meal Plan

This 28-day meal plan is designed to help you eliminate most of the foods that act as migraine triggers so that you can eventually start adding each food back in to determine whether it affects you. Each week includes the meal choices and convenient shopping lists to take the guesswork out of the process. The recipes for breakfast, lunch, dinner, and some of the snacks are found in part 3 of this book. If you elect not to make a particular recipe in the plan, simply replace it with another recipe in the book and adjust your shopping list accordingly.

The plan does not include desserts, so add those ingredients to the shopping lists if you want to try a treat or two. You will find leftovers incorporated into the plan as well as some instructions on how to double certain recipes. This duplication is to save time and also remain within a reasonable budget. The chicken and beef stock for the recipes can be made using the recipes in chapter 12, or you can purchase gluten-free products from the grocery store. If one of the choices includes an ingredient that is a migraine trigger for you, replace it with something appropriate and adjust the shopping list. This chart is also available for download at callistomedia.com /migrainereliefdiet.

		DAY 1	DAY 2	DAY 3	DAY 4	DAY 5	DAY 6	DAY 7
MORNING	Foods							
	Symptoms							
AFTERNOON	Foods							
	Symptoms							
EVENING	Foods							
	Symptoms							

THE
28-DAY
MEAL
PLAN

		DAY 1	DAY 2	DAY 3	DAY 4	DAY 5	DAY 6	DAY 7
MORNING	Foods							
	Symptoms							
AFTERNOON	Foods							
	Symptoms							
EVENING	Foods							
	Symptoms							

THE
28-DAY
MEAL
PLAN

		DAY 1	DAY 2	DAY 3	DAY 4	DAY 5	DAY 6	DAY 7
MORNING	Foods							
	Symptoms							
AFTERNOON	Foods							
	Symptoms							
EVENING	Foods							
	Symptoms							

THE
28-DAY
MEAL
PLAN

		DAY 1	DAY 2	DAY 3	DAY 4	DAY 5	DAY 6	DAY 7
MORNING	Foods							
	Symptoms							
AFTERNOON	Foods							
	Symptoms							
EVENING	Foods							
	Symptoms							

THE
28-DAY
MEAL
PLAN

THE 28-DAY MEAL PLAN WEEK 1

MONDAY

Breakfast: Watermelon–Basil
Smoothie (page 93)

Lunch: Chicken–Cabbage
Soup (page 119)

Dinner: Baked Tilapia with Bok Choy
and Spinach (page 126)

TUESDAY

Breakfast: Butternut Squash Breakfast
Casserole (page 100)

Lunch: Green Coleslaw (page 108)

Dinner: Juicy Meatloaf (page 140)

WEDNESDAY

Breakfast: Simple Turkey
Sausage (page 103)

Lunch: Juicy Meatloaf (leftovers)
(page 140)

Dinner: Chicken–Broccoli
Casserole (page 133)

THURSDAY

Breakfast: Sunny Carrot
Smoothie (page 92)

Lunch: Cheesy Kale Macaroni (page 164)

Dinner: Roasted Halibut with Bell
Pepper Salsa (page 122)

FRIDAY

Breakfast: Blueberry–Ricotta Pancakes
(double recipe for snack) (page 96)

Lunch: Shaved Brussels Sprout and
Herb Salad (page 106)

Dinner: Root Vegetable Stew (page 167)

SATURDAY

Breakfast: Green Pear
Smoothie (page 90)

Lunch: Melon Gazpacho with
Basil (page 112)

Dinner: Golden Roast
Chicken (page 134)

SUNDAY

Breakfast: Buckwheat Pancakes
with Nectarines (page 94)

Lunch: Waldorf Salad (with leftover
chicken) (page 111)

Dinner: Beef Brisket with Fall
Vegetables (page 143)

Suggested Snacks

Celery, cucumber, and carrot sticks

*Gluten-free pita bread with apple
and ricotta*

Grapes

Blueberry–Ricotta Pancakes (page 96)

Honeydew–Mint Ice Pops (page 187)

Colorful Veggie Salsa (page 174)

Mango Ice Cream (page 184)

WEEK 1 SHOPPING LIST

FRUITS AND VEGETABLES
Bartlett pear (1)
Blueberries (1 quart)
Bok choy (2 cups)
Broccoli (1 head)
Brussels sprouts
  (2 pounds)
Butternut squash
  (1½ pounds)
Cantaloupe (1)
Carrots (10)
Celery stalks (7)
Collard greens (1 pound)
English cucumbers (3)
Fennel bulb (1)
Granny Smith apples (5)
Green cabbage (1 head)
Green grapes (2 cups)
Horseradish (1 small knob)
Jicama (1)
Kale (14 ounces)
Leeks (5)
Mangos (2)
Napa cabbage (1 head)
Nectarines (4)
New potatoes (12)
Orange bell pepper (1)
Parsnips (5)
Potatoes (2)
Red bell pepper (3)
Scallions (5)
Shallots (16)
Spinach (1 pound)
Sweet potato (1)
Watermelon (1)

DAIRY, DAIRY ALTERNATIVES, AND EGGS
Cheese, ricotta (2 cups)
Cream cheese (1 cup)
Heavy (whipping)
  cream (1 cup)
Rice milk, unsweetened
  (4½ cups)

FRESH HERBS AND SPICES
Basil (1 bunch)
Cilantro (1 bunch)
Oregano (1 bunch)
Parsley (1 bunch)
Rosemary (1 bunch)
Thyme (1 bunch)

FISH AND SEAFOOD
Tilapia fillets (4, 8-ounce)
Halibut fillets (4, 6-ounce)

MEAT AND POULTRY
Beef brisket (1 pound)
Chicken breast, boneless,
  skinless (1½ pounds)
Chicken, whole roasting
  (1, 4-pound)
Ground beef, lean
  (2 pounds)
Ground turkey (1 pound)

PANTRY ITEMS
Arrowroot powder
Baking powder
Bay leaves
Black pepper,
  freshly ground

Breadcrumbs, gluten-free
Cayenne pepper, ground
Cinnamon, ground
Cloves, ground
Cumin, ground
Flour, buckwheat
Flour, rice
Flour, sweet white
  sorghum
Macaroni, gluten-free
Mustard, grainy
Nutmeg, ground
Nonstick olive oil
  cooking spray
Oil, coconut
Sea salt
Sunflower seeds
Vanilla extract, pure
Vinegar, white

OTHER
Dark Beef Stock (3 cups)
  (page 200)
Pita bread, gluten-free
  (1 package)
Potato starch (½ cup)
Simple Chicken Stock
  (8 cups) (page 199)
Stevia (3, 7g packets)
Vegetable stock, gluten-
  free (6 cups)
White rice (1½ cups)

WEEK 2 MEAL PLAN

MONDAY

Breakfast: Celeriac and Sweet Potato Pancakes (page 98)

Lunch: Beef Brisket with Fall Vegetables (leftovers) (page 143)

Dinner: Leek–Parsnip Soup (double batch) (page 117)

TUESDAY

Breakfast: Blueberry Green Smoothie (page 91)

Lunch: Leek–Parsnip Soup (leftovers) (page 117)

Dinner: Jambalaya (page 128)

WEDNESDAY

Breakfast: Butternut Squash Breakfast Casserole (page 100)

Lunch: Jambalaya (leftovers) (page 128)

Dinner: Salad Rolls with Mango–Ginger Sauce (page 146)

THURSDAY

Breakfast: Rice Pudding with Berries (page 192)

Lunch: Chickpea and Kale Soup (page 118)

Dinner: Beef Vegetable Stew (page 138)

FRIDAY

Breakfast: Watermelon–Basil Smoothie (page 93)

Lunch: Beef Vegetable Stew (leftovers) (page 138)

Dinner: Vegetarian Shepherd's Pie (page 162)

SATURDAY

Breakfast: Buckwheat Pancakes with Nectarines (page 94)

Lunch: Vegetarian Shepherd's Pie (leftovers) (page 162)

Dinner: Old-Fashioned "Battered" Fish (page 124)

SUNDAY

Breakfast: Sunny Carrot Smoothie (page 92)

Lunch: Vegetable Patties (double recipe) (page 152)

Dinner: Golden Roast Chicken (page 134)

Suggested Snacks

Watermelon slices

Nectarine

Gluten-free tortillas with cream cheese

Vegetable Patties (page 152)

Honeydew–Mint Ice Pops (page 187)

Roasted Red Pepper Dip (page 172)

Spiced Apple Chips (page 170)

WEEK 2 SHOPPING LIST

FRUITS AND VEGETABLES

Bean sprouts (½ cup)

Butternut squash
(1½ pounds)

Carrots (12)

Cauliflower (1 head)

Celeriac root (1)

Celery stalks (5)

English cucumbers (2)

Granny Smith apples (2)

Green cabbage (1 head)

Jicama (1)

Kale (14 ounces)

Leeks (11)

Lettuce, Boston (1)

Mangos (3)

Nectarines (5)

New potatoes (12)

Parsnips (10)

Red bell pepper (1)

Russet potatoes (6)

Scallions (6)

Shallots (20)

Spinach (1 pound)

Strawberries (1 quart)

Sweet potatoes (3)

Watermelon (1)

Yellow bell pepper (1)

Zucchini (1)

**DAIRY, DAIRY
ALTERNATIVES,
AND EGGS**

Cream cheese (1 cup)

Heavy (whipping) cream
(1¼ cups)

Rice milk, unsweetened
(1 half gallon)

**FRESH HERBS
AND SPICES**

Basil (1 bunch)

Cilantro (1 bunch)

Ginger (1, 3-inch knob)

Mint (1 bunch)

Parsley (1 bunch)

Rosemary (1 bunch)

Thyme (1 bunch)

FISH AND SEAFOOD

Haddock fillet, boneless,
skinless (1 pound)

Shrimp (16 to 20 count)

MEAT AND POULTRY

Beef chuck roast (1 pound)

Chicken breasts, boneless,
skinless (1 pound)

Chicken, whole roasting (1,
4-pound)

PANTRY ITEMS

Allspice, ground

Arrowroot powder

Baking powder

Bay leaves

Black pepper,
freshly ground

Cardamom, ground

Cayenne pepper, ground

Cinnamon, ground

Cloves, ground

Coriander, ground

Cumin, ground

Flour, buckwheat

Flour, rice

Nonstick olive oil
cooking spray

Nutmeg, ground

Oil, coconut

Paprika, ground

Red pepper flakes

Sea salt

Vanilla extract, pure

Vinegar, white

OTHER

Blueberries, frozen (1 cup)

Chickpeas, canned
(30 ounces)

Dark Beef Stock (5 cups)
(page 200)

Tortillas, gluten-free (4)

Potato starch (½ cup)

Simple Chicken Stock
(13 cups) (page 199)

Stevia (3, 7g) packets

Sushi rice (4 cups)

Vanilla bean (1)

Vegetable broth, gluten-
free (½ cup)

White rice (3 cups)

WEEK 3 MEAL PLAN

MONDAY

Breakfast: Homemade Applesauce (double batch) (page 182)

Lunch: Ginger–Chicken Wraps (with leftover chicken) (page 130)

Dinner: Quinoa–Stuffed Acorn Squash (page 148)

TUESDAY

Breakfast: Simple Turkey Sausage (page 103)

Lunch: Green Coleslaw (page 108)

Dinner: Juicy Meatloaf (page 140)

WEDNESDAY

Breakfast: Watermelon–Basil Smoothie (page 93)

Lunch: Juicy Meatloaf (leftovers) (page 140)

Dinner: Salmon with Creamy Leek Sauce (page 127)

THURSDAY

Breakfast: Blueberry–Ricotta Pancakes (page 96)

Lunch: Chicken–Cabbage Soup (double batch) (page 119)

Dinner: Beef Fajitas (page 141)

FRIDAY

Breakfast: Sunny Carrot Smoothie (page 92)

Lunch: Vegetable Fried Rice (page 150)

Dinner: Chicken–Cabbage Soup (leftovers) (page 119)

SATURDAY

Breakfast: Rice Pudding with Berries (page 192)

Lunch: Salad Rolls with Mango–Ginger Sauce (page 146)

Dinner: Roasted Halibut with Bell Pepper Salsa (page 122)

SUNDAY

Breakfast: Butternut Squash Breakfast Casserole (page 100)

Lunch: Kale and Herb Soup (page 113)

Dinner: Pumpkin Curry (page 165)

Suggested Snacks

Ricotta with grapes

Gluten-free crackers

Berries

Homemade Applesauce (page 182)

Peaches and Cream Ice Pops (page 186)

Cinnamon–Pear Leather (page 171)

Sweet Potato Fries (page 176)

WEEK 3 SHOPPING LIST

FRUITS AND VEGETABLES

Acorn squash (2)

Bean sprouts (½ cup)

Blueberries (1 quart)

Boston lettuce (2 heads)

Broccoli (1 head)

Butternut squash
(1½ pounds)

Carrots (4)

Celery stalks (2)

English cucumbers (2)

Fennel (1)

Granny Smith apples (15)

Green bell pepper (1)

Green cabbage (1 head)

Horseradish (1 small knob)

Jicama (2)

Kale (12 ounces)

Leeks (12)

Mangos (3)

Napa cabbage (1 head)

Orange bell pepper (1)

Parsnip (1)

Potatoes (2)

Pumpkin (1)

Red bell pepper (5)

Scallions (7)

Shallots (7)

Strawberries (1 quart)

Swiss chard (5 ounces)

Watermelon (1)

Zucchini (1)

DAIRY, DAIRY ALTERNATIVES, AND EGGS

Cheese, ricotta (1½ cups)

Heavy (whipping) cream
(2 cups)

Rice milk, unsweetened
(3 cups)

FRESH HERBS AND SPICES

Basil (1 bunch)

Cilantro (1 bunch)

Ginger (1, 6-inch knob)

Mint (1 bunch)

Oregano (1 bunch)

Parsley (1 bunch)

Thyme (1 bunch)

FISH AND SEAFOOD

Halibut fillets (4, 6 ounces)

Salmon fillet (1½ pounds)

MEAT AND POULTRY

Chicken breast, boneless,
skinless (2 pounds)

Flank steak (1 pound)

Ground beef, lean
(2 pounds)

Ground turkey (1 pound)

PANTRY ITEMS

Allspice, ground

Arrowroot powder

Baking powder

Bay leaves

Black pepper,
freshly ground

Breadcrumbs, gluten-free

Cinnamon, ground

Cloves, ground

Coriander, ground

Cumin, ground

Curry powder

Flour, rice

Flour, sweet
white sorghum

Nonstick olive oil
cooking spray

Nutmeg, ground

Oil, coconut

Sea salt

Turmeric, ground

Vinegar, white

OTHER

Chickpeas, canned
(8 ounces)

Quinoa (1 cup)

Simple Chicken Stock
(4¼ cups) (page 199)

Stevia (9, 7g packets)

Tortillas, gluten-free (4)

Vanilla bean (1)

Vegetable stock, gluten-
free (2 cups)

White rice (2½ cups)

WEEK 4 MEAL PLAN

MONDAY

Breakfast: Watermelon–Basil Smoothie (page 93)

Lunch: Pumpkin Curry (leftovers) (page 165)

Dinner: Grilled Lamb Chops with Mint Pesto (page 136)

TUESDAY

Breakfast: Simple Turkey Sausage (page 103)

Lunch: Jicama–Melon Salad with Cucumber Dressing (page 109)

Dinner: Golden Roast Chicken (page 134)

WEDNESDAY

Breakfast: Blueberry–Ricotta Pancakes (page 96)

Lunch: Waldorf Salad (with leftover chicken) (page 111)

Dinner: Baked Tilapia with Bok Choy and Spinach (page 126)

THURSDAY

Breakfast: Green Pear Smoothie (page 90)

Lunch: Quinoa Tabbouleh (page 156)

Dinner: Beef Vegetable Stew (page 138)

FRIDAY

Breakfast: Rice Pudding with Berries (page 192)

Lunch: Beef Vegetable Stew (leftovers) (page 138)

Dinner: Classic Colcannon (page 161)

SATURDAY

Breakfast: Buckwheat Pancakes with Nectarines (page 94)

Lunch: Broccoli and Rice Soup (page 115)

Dinner: Roasted Halibut with Bell Pepper Salsa (page 122)

SUNDAY

Breakfast: Blueberry Panna Cotta (page 185)

Lunch: Salad Rolls with Mango–Ginger Sauce (page 146)

Dinner: Chicken–Broccoli Casserole (page 133)

Suggested Snacks

Crudité (carrots, cucumber, broccoli)

Granny Smith apple

Watermelon slices

Gluten-free bagel with cream cheese

Peaches and Cream Ice Pops (page 186)

Pumpkin Hummus (page 173)

Cinnamon–Pear Leather (page 171)

FRUITS AND VEGETABLES

Bartlett pear (1)

Bean sprouts (½ cup)

Blueberries (1 quart)

Bok choy (2 cups)

Boston lettuce (1 head)

Broccoli (2 heads)

Cantaloupe (1)

Carrots (5)

Celery stalks (10)

English cucumbers (4)

Granny Smith apples (2)

Green cabbage (1 head)

Green grapes (2 cups)

Honeydew melon (1)

Jicama (3)

Kale (16 ounces)

Leeks (2)

Mangos (2)

Nectarines (5)

Orange bell pepper (1)

Parsnips (2)

Radishes (4)

Red bell pepper (3)

Russet potato (5)

Scallions (6)

Shallots (12)

Spinach (12 ounces)

Strawberries (1 quart)

Watermelon (1)

DAIRY, DAIRY ALTERNATIVES, AND EGGS

Cheese, ricotta (1 cup)

Heavy (whipping) cream (3 cups)

Rice milk, unsweetened (6 cups)

FRESH HERBS AND SPICES

Basil (1 bunch)

Ginger (1, 2-inch knob)

Mint (1 bunch)

Oregano (1 bunch)

Parsley (1 bunch)

Rosemary (1 bunch)

Thyme (1 bunch)

FISH AND SEAFOOD

Halibut fillets (4, 6-ounce)

Tilapia fillets (4, 8-ounce)

MEAT AND POULTRY

Beef chuck roast (1 pound)

Chicken breast, boneless, skinless (2 pounds)

Chicken, whole roasting (1, 4-pound)

Ground turkey (1 pound)

Lamb loin chops (8)

PANTRY

Allspice, ground

Arrowroot powder

Baking powder

Black pepper, freshly ground

Cinnamon, ground

Cloves, ground

Coriander, ground

Cumin, ground

Flour, Buckwheat

Flour, rice

Flour, sweet white sorghum

Nonstick olive oil cooking spray

Nutmeg, ground

Oil, coconut

Red pepper flakes

Sea salt

Sunflower seeds

Vanilla extract, pure

Vinegar, white

OTHER

Brown rice (1½ cups)

Dark Beef Stock (5 cups) (page 200)

Gelatin leaves (3)

Potato starch (½ cup)

Simple Chicken Stock (8 cups) (page 199)

Stevia (6, 7g packets)

Vanilla bean (1)

White rice (3 cups)

TIME-SAVING STRATEGIES

There are certain strategies you can employ to minimize the stress involved in following a new diet. You might initially feel overwhelmed when you think about preparing every single meal and snack yourself for the next month, but with a few tips and tricks, you can easily put together healthy, nutritious meals in the same amount of time it would take you to visit your local cafe for lunch. The following tips will help you prepare all of your meals quickly and easily.

- **Devote time to preparing meals on the weekend.** On a Sunday night, prepare as much of your food for the week ahead as possible. You can roast meat to store in the fridge or freezer, wash and cut fruits and vegetables, cook starchy carbohydrates such as rice, quinoa, and potatoes, and prepare a large portion of broth or sauce. Roasting meat and vegetables is generally the easiest cooking method. For example, when you already have the oven switched on to bake chicken breasts, it requires minimal extra effort to roast some vegetables at the same time. If your meat and grains are already prepared, it will take only moments to throw together a healthy meal.

- **Make friends with your slow cooker.** As previously mentioned, a slow cooker will save you time. It takes just 10 minutes to put some meat, vegetables, and stock in a slow cooker at the start of the day. By the time you get home from work, you will have six to eight portions of food waiting for you.

- **Keep snacks simple.** Devote the majority of your effort to preparing your three main meals, and stick to simple, fast snacks such as hardboiled eggs, seeds, and fruits. As part of your weekly food preparation, you can chop and portion out some vegetables to have on hand as snacks. In addition, you can try making a batch of Rice Pudding with Berries (page 192) or Peaches and Cream Ice Pops (page 186).

Managing Expectations

As you work your way through these meal plans, you can expect to see a number of both positive and negative physical effects. Depending on what your diet consisted of prior to starting these plans, you should feel as though you have more energy, improved digestion, less hunger, fewer mood fluctuations, and better hair, nails, and skin. You may also experience weight loss and, of course, a reduction in the severity and intensity of your migraine attacks.

However, it is also normal to sometimes experience headaches, cravings, and decreased energy levels when you initially embark upon the plan, until all the toxins and addictive substances have completely exited your body.

Positive Changes

You may experience any or all of the following positive effects, either immediately or after a week or two of following the *Migraine Relief Diet*. Provided you stick with this new type of diet for the foreseeable future, you will continue to experience these benefits over the long term.

Better Digestion You can expect your digestion to improve, with a reduction in bloating, constipation, and diarrhea alongside an increase in regularity. Many people are unaware of how sensitive they may be to foods such as gluten and dairy. It is not until they remove these foods from their diets that they realize how much better they can feel. The meal plan contains a great deal of fiber, which will also have a positive effect on your bowel movements. Finally, this type of diet will improve your gut flora and decrease inflammation within the digestive tract.

Fewer and Less Intense Migraines Most importantly, you will likely begin to suffer from migraines less frequently, and when they do occur, they should be much less severe. This diet is optimized to keep dietary triggers to a minimum, which will reduce your chance of a migraine episode.

Improved Hair, Nails, and Skin Increasing your intake of healthy fats as outlined in the preceding meal plans may increase the quality of your hair and nails, which should become stronger and less prone to breakage. If you have any skin problems such as dryness or acne, you will likely see an improvement in your condition. This is due to the reduced amount of foods containing artificial hormones in your diet as well as an increase in fats and reduction in high-glycemic foods.

Increased Energy Most Americans eat a diet full of processed, high-sugar foods, and they often rely on regular bursts of caffeine to make it through the day. When you eliminate these foods, you might be surprised at how energetic you feel. You may find yourself waking up without the help of caffeine, and as your energy levels remain constant throughout the day, you may no longer experience a mid-afternoon energy slump. Your sleep should also improve.

Steady Blood Sugar Levels When you eat processed foods, your blood sugar levels rise and fall dramatically. Switching to the type of diet promoted in these meal plans will help keep your energy levels stable. The foods in the plans will release energy slowly and evenly into your blood stream, and hunger will develop gradually and naturally. You will rarely feel the type of hunger that can leave you diving head-first into the cookie jar. You may also find that your concentration improves and you become less irritable.

Weight Loss Although the intention of this diet is not to lose weight, that can be a natural side effect. Again, if your diet previously consisted of a lot of unhealthy "junk" foods—which are high in calories and low in nutrients—it is natural for you to lose weight immediately after you commence this plan.

Negative Changes

As not everyone will be following the same style of eating before commencing the *Migraine Relief Diet*, not everyone will experience all or even any of these negative symptoms. However, it is important that you are aware of what may occur so that you can be better prepared and less inclined to throw in the towel. The good news is that these negative changes are only temporary, and most will subside within a matter of days.

Cravings Many of the foods you will be eliminating are addictive. Not only does this mean your body will initially be in shock from a physiological point of view, but it also means you are likely to struggle with cravings for off-plan foods. Cakes, ice cream, and potato chips will suddenly become incredibly tempting when you know that you can't have them.

Cravings are completely normal. Keep the trigger foods out of arm's reach, and make sure you have healthy snacks on hand. If you are desperate for something sweet, try any of the recommended fruits or herbal tea. The good news is that once your body has removed the toxins from its bloodstream, your body will naturally stop craving these "bad" foods. In fact, when you inevitably consume these types of foods again, you may find you no longer enjoy the taste of them.

Decreased Energy Despite an increase in energy levels once you commence this diet, initially, you might feel tired. This is a symptom of withdrawal and is simply your body's reaction to losing energy from processed, chemically laden foods. Your energy levels should perk up within a few short days, and you will likely feel more energetic than you were before starting the elimination diet.

Headaches Both caffeine and sugar contain addictive properties. If you have been consuming substantial amounts of these substances and then suddenly quit them both, cold turkey, during the 3-day cleanse, you may go through a period of withdrawal. During this time, you may suffer from headaches (which can then progress to migraines), a general feeling of fatigue, and even muscular aches and pains. This withdrawal period typically lasts up to three days.

Chapter Five

Reintroduction

Once you have completed the 28-day meal plan, you can safely begin reintroducing some trigger foods into your diet. You might find that you are able to reincorporate some of your favorite foods into your life, but you might also find that you function best without them.

Personally, no matter how hard I try to fight it, I can never eat dairy or certain processed meats without suffering a bad reaction. On rare occasions, I do eat these foods, but I know that I have no one to blame but myself if I end up with a migraine. As much as I miss salami and ice cream, the pain associated with consuming these foods is simply not worth it. For me, living a healthy and fulfilling life almost free of migraines is more important, even if it means avoiding foods I enjoy.

The reintroduction phase is crucial, as there is no need to limit certain foods in your diet—and therefore potentially miss out on important nutrients—if you have no reason to. You will continue to closely track your migraines and other symptoms as you reintroduce each trigger food slowly and sensibly, as outlined in the following pages. You will then be able to identify those foods that are problematic for you—and those that are safe.

The reintroduction stage can be painful, and it can be difficult to purposely consume foods you may believe to be triggers. However, one day of discomfort is worth it to know whether you need to restrict a certain food from your diet for the rest of your life.

You may find that consuming small amounts of a certain trigger food causes no adverse problems. You may also find that your tolerance for certain foods varies according to numerous other factors; for example, female hormones vary over the course of the month, and that can make some food triggers—such as chocolate—more likely to cause migraines at certain times.

This phase of the plan may take several months. It cannot be rushed, as you risk negating all your hard work from the elimination stage. You must reintroduce each food one at a time, and sometimes multiple times, to confirm a reaction, which can be time consuming. You may find that what acts as a trigger now may not present problems in the future, and vice versa, so the link between your diet and migraine episodes is one you must monitor for the rest of your life.

Understanding how diet affects you involves a lot of personal experimentation and a great deal of time and patience. It can be a difficult but also empowering process. Use the following plan to guide you through this final, yet crucial, stage.

Safe Reintroduction

Although it can be tempting to immediately gorge yourself on all the forbidden foods at once after completing the 28-day plan, you must approach the reintroduction phase sensibly by following the steps below. The process itself is simple, but it requires some discipline.

It is important to not get your hopes up too much; there is a very real chance that many of the foods you eliminated during the 3-day cleanse and 28-day plan will indeed prove to be migraine triggers for you, meaning that you will not be able to eat them again if you wish to remain healthy. Accept that this diet involves a long-term lifestyle change and that any permanent eliminations are a small sacrifice to make in the name of optimal health.

One Food at a Time

Although this will be time consuming, it is crucial that you only reintroduce one food at a time. This way you will be able to determine exactly how your body responds to that food and that food only. For example, if you reintroduce processed meats, dairy, and gluten all at the same time in the form of a pizza, and subsequently suffer a migraine, it will be unclear which ingredient in that meal was responsible. It is important to consume foods in their purest forms, such as eating an orange rather than drinking orange juice.

Remember to track your migraine symptoms closely using the Reintroduction Symptom Tracker (page 85) so you can identify which foods act as triggers for you.

Start with Small Amounts

It is important not to get carried away when reintroducing a potential trigger food. If you decide to reintroduce dairy, do not have a yogurt bowl followed by a milk shake followed by a pint of ice cream. Instead, try having half a cup of yogurt and monitoring how your body responds. Then, next time, try having a slightly larger serving. Sometimes you will be able to tolerate small amounts of a certain trigger food, so it is important to make note of your portion sizes.

If you have a negative reaction at any point in this process, stop eating that food immediately and make a note that it is probably a trigger for you.

Wait Three Days

Just because you are not immediately struck down by a migraine does not mean that particular food is not a trigger for you. Each food should be reintroduced and monitored over a three-day period. Eat the particular food on day one only, and then wait three days for any delayed symptoms to manifest themselves while adhering to your regular elimination diet.

If you have any kind of negative reaction, be sure to wait until all of your symptoms have subsided by following the original elimination diet before consuming the next potential trigger food.

Consume the Food Daily

If you do not experience a negative reaction at any point within the three-day period, then try consuming a small amount of the trigger food each day. Sometimes you will require a prolonged exposure to a certain food for it to produce a negative reaction. This means that you can consume the food occasionally, under certain conditions. From there, it will be your decision whether to reincorporate the food into your diet on a regular basis.

If you do not have a negative reaction after repeated exposure, the food is not a trigger for you and can be permanently added back into your diet. You can now move on to the next potential culprit, repeating the steps above.

Try Different Foods Within Each Category

Just because you had a bad reaction to beets, for example, does not mean that all vegetables containing tyramine will be a trigger for you. Repeat the reintroduction process with *all* of the foods listed within each category before eliminating an entire food group.

For example, I haven't had any issues with bacon and deli ham, but other processed meats such as salami and sausages are usually triggers for me. It would have been easy for me to assume that all processed meats were triggers based on my initial reaction to two types, when in reality I can tolerate certain variations just fine.

Give Foods a Second Chance

Remember, just because a certain food is a trigger does not mean that it alone will be enough to cross your migraine threshold. For instance, you may try reintroducing dairy only to end up with a migraine. Rather than immediately assume it must be a strong trigger, consider what other factors may be involved. Were you also exposed to bright lights? Did you sleep poorly the night before? Are you under an extraordinary amount of stress? Take the offending food out for a week or two, and then try eating it again. If it causes another reaction, you can more firmly confirm it as a trigger.

Even if you experience two or more negative reactions to a certain food, that may not mean you need to banish it from your diet for eternity. Six months, one year, or even five years down the line, you can try again. For example, I used to almost always suffer migraines after drinking red wine, and this was the case for many years. However, now that I have learned to better manage my other migraine triggers, I seem to be able to tolerate one or two glasses without any problem.

Which Foods to Reintroduce First

Just as the process of adding trigger foods back into your diet is careful and deliberate, so is the process of determining exactly which foods to reintroduce first. You will begin with those that are least problematic for the majority of migraineurs—thereby keeping pain to a minimum—as well as those that contain the most nutritional value.

Starting with vegetables, proceed through the list as follows, working through the principles of safe introduction as outlined above. Remember that you should reintroduce foods one at a time, rather than an entire category of food at once. This is because you may be able to eat butter and cream but not milk or cheese, for example.

Vegetables

As they are the most nutrient-dense food group that has been eliminated from your diet, the vegetables you have been avoiding should be the first to be reintroduced. This includes vegetables such as beets, chile peppers, eggplants, string beans, garlic, and onions. These vegetables should be reintroduced one at a time, in no particular order, following the process previously outlined.

Corn is one final vegetable that may be reintroduced, provided it is in its natural form and not as corn syrup.

Fruits

Next, you may reintroduce avocados, bananas, cranberries, pineapples, tangerines, and citrus fruits. Reintroduce one citrus fruit at a time. Lemon and lime may be squeezed into mineral water, while oranges and grapefruits should be eaten whole.

Nuts

You may now reintroduce all kinds of nuts, one at the time, including almonds, Brazil nuts, cashews, macadamia nuts, peanuts, pine nuts, and walnuts.

Fermented Foods

You may now try adding foods such as pickles, sauerkraut, and smoked mackerel. Again, you may simply reintroduce these in the order of which foods you have missed the most, and there is no need to reintroduce foods you would not eat under normal conditions.

Processed Meats

Next, in the order of your choice, reintroduce bacon, ham, salami, and sausage. If any of these foods cause problems, it will be sensible to stick to unprocessed forms of meat in the future.

Dairy

Dairy can be problematic as it not only contains casein but many forms also contain tyramine. Therefore, it is best not to reintroduce dairy products right away. Once you have made your way through the preceding list, start your dairy reintroduction with more easily digestible forms such as milk and butter before moving on to foods like yogurt or hard cheeses. You may also wish to test different types of cheeses on different days, since you may respond negatively to one type but not another. Some people may also tolerate raw but not pasteurized dairy, and vice versa.

Chocolate

Chocolate is problematic because it contains not only caffeine, but also sugar, and should therefore be limited. That said, many people have a hard time letting go of this sweet treat. In that case, simply limit your indulgences to a couple of times per week, and opt for dark chocolate wherever possible, as it contains a higher percentage of cocoa and less sugar.

Gluten

Remember, gluten can be problematic for a number of reasons unrelated to migraines. Therefore, even though you may not find gluten to be a personal migraine trigger, you may feel better eliminating it from your diet anyway. Many foods with gluten also contain other ingredients that have been eliminated, hence it is important to make it one of the final foods in the reintroduction process. Be sure to test each type of gluten grain (wheat, barley, and rye) separately.

Soy

Like gluten, soy can also be problematic for many people outside of its role as a migraine trigger, so it may be best left out of your diet permanently. Start by adding some soy sauce to your food or snacking on a few pieces of edamame to see if it has a negative effect.

Alcohol

Alcohol is the final substance you will reintroduce. Wine, beer, and hard liquor should be tested on different days, as the reaction to each may be different. Limit yourself to just one glass initially.

Foods You Won't Reintroduce

Some foods are best left out of your diet permanently due to the damaging effects they have on your body. This includes artificial sweeteners, caffeine, MSG, and sugar. Hopefully by now you will no longer be missing these foods, so it will be easier to keep them out of your diet completely—or at least save them for very occasional indulgences. These foods offer no nutritional benefits, so you will not be lacking anything by leaving them out of your diet.

Artificial Sweeteners

Sweeteners contain artificial ingredients that are best kept out of your system. They affect your blood sugar levels and can in turn cause weight gain, as well as increase your risk of type 2 diabetes.

Caffeine

Remember that caffeine itself is not a migraine trigger; rather, it is the physical dependency you develop with regard to the substance that is the problem. It is therefore important to continue to eliminate caffeine, or at least restrict the amount you consume. Some can tolerate one cup of coffee per week, but determining whether you are one of those people will involve some personal experimentation. Only do this once you have attempted to reintroduce all other potential triggers from the approved list.

MSG

MSG is well known for having a negative impact on your health, as it is linked not only to migraines but also abdominal cramping, diarrhea, sweating, and chest pain. It is best avoided.

Sugar

Although it is almost impossible to eliminate sugar completely, your consumption of it can, and should, be limited. Remember that sugar has a negative effect on blood sugar levels and, in turn, blood pressure. It also increases your chance of weight gain, diabetes, and heart disease.

Tracking Your Symptoms

As you reintroduce the aforementioned foods, it is extremely important to keep track of how your body responds by recording all reactions and symptoms using the Reintroduction Symptom Tracker (page 85). This way, you will be able to clearly identify the triggers that are and are not problematic for you. This chart is also online at calistomedia.com/migrainereliefdiet.

Firstly, make a clear note of which food you have reintroduced. Keep track of how you feel, whether that may be positive or negative. Monitor your sleep, mood, energy, digestion, and bowel movements. Also make note of any other events occurring in your life, so you know whether your sleep or stress levels, for example, may be to blame for any reactions rather than a particular food.

Reintroduction FAQs

Now that you are armed with the information you'll need to complete the reintroduction phase, it is likely you have some questions. Here are answers to some of the most common questions people have when commencing this stage of the process.

If I react to a food, should I eliminate it forever? The human body is a complex, dynamic system. Just because you have a negative reaction to a certain food now does not mean that you always will. If you respond negatively to a certain food, wait three to six months and try again.

What if I react to one food in a category but not another? It is perfectly normal to experience a negative reaction to one food within a particular category but not another. This is why it is crucial to work your way through each food one at a time, rather than attempting to reintroduce an entire food group all at once. You will therefore be able to eat some foods within a particular category but not others.

Do I have to follow this diet forever? Don't think of this as a temporary diet but rather a lifestyle change. No one will force you to follow this diet forever; however, you will likely feel significantly better if you stay away from your personal trigger foods on a long-term basis. At the end of the day, you will have to make a choice between your health and food, and you have to decide what's best for you. Many people report that the health benefits gained from keeping certain foods out of their diet make all forms of elimination worthwhile.

Reintroduction Symptom Tracker / Weekly Meal Plan   Week __

		DAY 1	DAY 2	DAY 3	DAY 4	DAY 5	DAY 6	DAY 7
MORNING	Foods							
	Symptoms							
AFTERNOON	Foods							
	Symptoms							
EVENING	Foods							
	Symptoms							

One of the hardest things about starting a diet is finding suitable recipes for your goals that also taste delicious and that you don't have to break your budget to create. The recipes in this section include many ingredients that can be found in your local grocery store, with no trouble. You don't need any special equipment, either.

The goal of the *Migraine Relief Diet* is to help you manage and reduce the frequency of your migraines. The ingredients in each recipe are designed to eliminate all the common migraine triggers as well as some common food allergens. However, because every person is different and migraine triggers can be very specific, remember to replace any ingredient that causes you discomfort with another that works for you. Most cooking is not an exact science, so enjoy the process and savor the results.

PART

3

THE RECIPES

Chapter Six

Breakfasts

Green Pear Smoothie

Serves 2 / Prep time: 5 minutes

Bartlett pears, otherwise known as Williams pears, are the most commonly grown green pears in North America. These pears change color from green to a lovely yellow as they brighten and are best eaten in the fall and early winter. Pears are members of the rose family, and Bartletts are famous for their characteristic "pear" shape and buttery-smooth texture when ripe.

NUT-FREE

VEGAN

QUICK &
EASY

2 cups kale

1 ripe Bartlett pear, cored and chopped

½ English cucumber, cut into chunks

1 tablespoon sunflower seeds

½ teaspoon ground cinnamon

½ teaspoon ground nutmeg

4 ice cubes

1. In a blender, blend the kale, pear, cucumber, sunflower seeds, cinnamon, and nutmeg until smooth.

2. Add the ice, and blend until smooth and thick.

3. Pour the smoothie into 2 glasses, and serve.

Allergy Adjustments: *Some people are sensitive to seeds. So if you have issues with this food product, omit the sunflower seeds from the smoothie.*

PER SERVING Calories: 91; Total Fat: 1g; Saturated Fat: 0g; Cholesterol: 0mg; Total Carbohydrates: 21g; Fiber: 4g; Protein: 3g

Blueberry Green Smoothie

Serves 2 / Prep time: 15 minutes

Spinach is the perfect choice for your breakfast smoothie because it is packed with many nutrients such as riboflavin, which can help boost energy metabolism in the cells and brain. Many migraine sufferers have impaired energy function in these areas. You can also substitute kale, Swiss chard, or other dark leafy greens if they suit your palate better or you happen to have them in your refrigerator. If you want to use fresh blueberries, add a couple of ice cubes to create a pleasing thick texture.

1 cup frozen blueberries

1 mango, peeled, pitted, and chopped

½ cup English cucumber, cut into chunks

2 cups spinach

½ cup water

1. In a blender, blend the blueberries, mango, cucumber, spinach, and water until thick and smooth.
2. Pour the smoothie into 2 glasses, and serve.

PER SERVING Calories: 125; Total Fat: 1g; Saturated Fat: 0g; Cholesterol: 0mg; Total Carbohydrates: 30g; Fiber: 4g; Protein: 2g

NUT-FREE

VEGAN

QUICK & EASY

Sunny Carrot Smoothie

Serves 2 / Prep time: 5 minutes

NUT-FREE

VEGAN

QUICK &
EASY

This smoothie is absolutely packed with beta-carotene from the bright carrots and ripe mango. Mangos have an interesting, almost pine-like taste, which combines beautifully with the thyme in this pretty breakfast drink. Mangos are an excellent source of vitamins A, B$_6$, and C, as well as fiber and potassium. When choosing your mangos, look beyond the color, and pick fruit that gives when you press it gently and has a delicate scent near the stem end. To blanch vegetables, simply cook them in boiling water before plunging them in ice water.

2 large carrots, peeled, cut into chunks, and blanched for 5 minutes
1 Granny Smith apple, cored and cut into chunks
1 mango, peeled, pitted, and cut into chunks
½ English cucumber, cut into chunks
½ teaspoon chopped fresh thyme
4 ice cubes

1. In a blender, blend the carrots, apple, mango, cucumber, and thyme until smooth.

2. Add the ice cubes, and blend until thick and smooth.

3. Pour the mixture into 2 glasses, and serve.

PER SERVING Calories: 161; Total Fat: 1g; Saturated Fat: 0g; Cholesterol: 0mg;
Total Carbohydrates: 40g; Fiber: 6g; Protein: 2g

Watermelon-Basil Smoothie

Serves 2 / Prep time: 15 minutes

Dehydration can be a contributing factor in migraines, and watermelon has a very high water content. Try to leave some of the pale green flesh found between the rind and red parts of the melon, because this area contains most of the antioxidants. Don't worry; this green area will not detract from the sweetness of the smoothie. Do not substitute red cabbage for the green variety because the red vegetable contains tannins, which can be a migraine trigger.

3 cups cubed watermelon

½ cup green cabbage

¼ English cucumber, cut into chunks

2 tablespoons chopped fresh basil

4 or 5 ice cubes

1. In a blender, blend the watermelon, cabbage, cucumber, and basil until the mixture is smooth.

2. Add the ice cubes, and blend until thick and smooth.

3. Pour the mixture into 2 glasses, and serve.

PER SERVING Calories: 74; Total Fat: 0g; Saturated Fat: 0g; Cholesterol: 0mg; Total Carbohydrates: 18g; Fiber: 2g; Protein: 2g

NUT-FREE

VEGAN

QUICK &
EASY

Buckwheat Pancakes with Nectarines

Serves 4 / Prep time: 10 minutes / Cook time: 20 minutes

NUT-FREE

VEGAN

QUICK & EASY

You might be wondering how an ingredient with "wheat" in its name is gluten-free, but buckwheat is not a grain at all; it is actually a fruit seed. You can find buckwheat flour in most grocery stores, especially in the organic sections, in both light and dark varieties. Both types will be delicious in this recipe, but the darker flour is more nutritious. Keep your unused buckwheat flour in the refrigerator in a sealed container.

2 cups buckwheat flour

½ cup potato starch

2 teaspoons baking powder

½ teaspoon salt

2 cups unsweetened rice milk

¼ cup coconut oil, melted

2 teaspoons pure vanilla extract

Nonstick olive oil cooking spray

4 cups sliced nectarines, for serving

1. In a large bowl, stir together the buckwheat, potato starch, baking powder, and salt.

2. In a small bowl, whisk together the milk, oil, and vanilla.

3. Stir the wet ingredients into the dry ingredients until the batter is smooth.

4. Place a large skillet over medium-high heat, and spray it lightly with the cooking spray.

5. Working in batches as needed, spoon the batter into the skillet to form 4 pancakes, about ¼ cup of batter per pancake.

6. Cook until bubbles appear on the surface of the pancakes, about 3 minutes.

7. Using a spatula, flip the pancakes over, and cook the other side until golden brown, about 2 minutes.

8. Repeat with the remaining batter.

9. Serve the pancakes topped with the nectarines.

PER SERVING Calories: 582; Total Fat: 18g; Saturated Fat: 12g; Cholesterol: 0mg; Total Carbohydrates: 91g; Fiber: 15g; Protein: 12g

Blueberry-Ricotta Pancakes

Serves 4 / Prep time: 15 minutes / Cook time: 15 minutes

Ricotta cheese was originally created from the whey left over after Italian cheese makers produced mozzarella and provolone. This mild, sweet, fresh cheese is now made from pasteurized milk with added salt and vinegar. Ricotta is often confused with cottage cheese, but there are significant differences. For example, ricotta has about 5 times more calcium than cottage cheese. Fresh fruit, such as the blueberries in these golden pancakes, is a wonderful accompaniment for this creamy, firm cheese.

NUT-FREE

VEGETARIAN

QUICK &
EASY

1 cup sweet white sorghum flour
1 cup rice flour
1 tablespoon baking powder
1 (7g) stevia packet
¼ teaspoon sea salt
1 cup ricotta cheese
½ cup heavy (whipping) cream
2 cups fresh blueberries
2 tablespoons coconut oil, divided

1. In a large bowl, stir together the sorghum flour, rice flour, baking powder, stevia, and salt until well blended.

2. In a small bowl, whisk together the ricotta and cream.

3. Add the wet ingredients to the dry ingredients, and stir to blend.

4. Stir in the blueberries.

5. In a large skillet over medium-high heat, heat 1 tablespoon of coconut oil.

6. Spoon the batter, about ½ cup for each pancake, into the skillet. You should have room for 4 pancakes.

7. Cook the pancakes until the bottoms are golden and the edges are firm, about 4 minutes.

8. Using a spatula, flip the pancakes over, and cook the other sides until golden, about 4 minutes.

9. Transfer the pancakes to a plate, and repeat with the remaining 1 tablespoon of coconut oil and the remaining batter.

10. Serve.

PER SERVING Calories: 506; Total Fat: 19g; Saturated Fat: 13g; Cholesterol: 40mg; Total Carbohydrates: 73g; Fiber: 6g; Protein: 14g

Celeriac and Sweet Potato Pancakes

Serves 5 / Prep time: 20 minutes / Cook time: 30 minutes

NUT-FREE

VEGAN

If you are a fan of lacy golden latkes or hash browns, this recipe might become a new favorite dish. The trick to a perfect shredded vegetable pancake is to leave it alone while it fries in the oil so that a crispy crust forms on the bottom and the center cooks through while remaining tender. Do not lift the pancakes until you see the edges turn golden and set.

1 celeriac root, peeled and shredded (about 6 cups)
2 small sweet potatoes, peeled and shredded (about 4 cups)
¼ cup chopped shallots
2 tablespoons arrowroot powder
1 teaspoon chopped fresh thyme
½ teaspoon sea salt
¼ teaspoon freshly ground black pepper
Nonstick olive oil cooking spray
Sautéed apples or applesauce, for serving

1. Squeeze out as much liquid as possible from the celeriac and sweet potatoes, and put the vegetables in a large bowl.

2. Stir the shallots, arrowroot, thyme, salt, and pepper into the shredded vegetables until well combined.

3. Place a large skillet over medium heat, and spray it generously with cooking spray.

4. Add 1 cup of the shredded vegetable mixture per pancake to the skillet, and press the mixture down with a spatula. Three pancakes should fit at one time.

5. Cook the pancakes until the bottoms are golden and crispy, about 5 minutes.

6. Using a spatula, flip the pancakes over, and cook the other side until golden and crispy, about 5 minutes.

7. Transfer the finished pancakes to a paper towel–lined plate.

8. Repeat with the remaining shredded vegetable mixture.

9. Serve 2 pancakes per person, topping with sautéed apples or applesauce.

How It Helps: *Sweet potatoes are packed with migraine-fighting magnesium and are an effective antioxidant. They are also very unlikely to cause an allergic reaction of any kind.*

PER SERVING Calories: 170; Total Fat: 1g; Saturated Fat: 0g; Cholesterol: 0mg; Total Carbohydrates: 39g; Fiber: 6g; Protein: 4g

Butternut Squash Breakfast Casserole

Serves 4 / Prep time: 15 minutes / Cook time: 1 hour, 20 minutes

NUT-FREE

VEGAN

Nothing beats a tempting casserole that can be put together the night before and baked with no mess or fuss in the morning. If you want to bake it straight from the refrigerator, then increase the cooking time by about 25 minutes to ensure everything is warmed through. A handful of shredded kale or spinach is a nice addition if you want to boost the migraine-fighting magnesium in this dish.

Nonstick olive oil cooking spray
1 butternut squash (about 1½ pounds), peeled, halved, and seeded
1 tablespoon coconut oil
1 cup chopped leeks, washed
1 large carrot, shredded
1 Granny Smith apple, peeled, cored, and chopped
½ teaspoon sea salt
¼ teaspoon freshly ground black pepper
¼ teaspoon ground nutmeg
Pinch ground cloves
1 cup unsweetened rice milk

1. Preheat the oven to 350°F.
2. Lightly spray a 9-by-13-inch baking dish with cooking spray, and set aside.
3. Cut the squash halves lengthwise into 4 wedges each. Halve the wedges across the width, and transfer the pieces to a large bowl.
4. In a large skillet over medium-high heat, heat the coconut oil.

5. Sauté the leeks until they are tender, about 5 minutes. Set aside.

6. In the large bowl with the squash, toss together the carrot, apple, salt, pepper, nutmeg, and cloves, combining well with the squash.

7. Transfer half of the squash mixture to the baking dish, and spread the mixture out evenly.

8. Top the squash layer with the cooked leeks, and top the leeks with the remaining squash mixture.

9. Pour the milk evenly into the baking dish, cover the casserole with foil, and bake for 1 hour.

10. Remove the foil, and bake the casserole for 15 minutes more.

11. Let the casserole sit for 10 minutes before serving.

PER SERVING Calories: 149; Total Fat: 4g; Saturated Fat: 3g; Cholesterol: 0mg; Total Carbohydrates: 30g; Fiber: 6g; Protein: 2g

Chicken and Pumpkin Hash

Serves 4 / Prep time: 10 minutes / Cook time: 30 minutes

NUT-FREE

Chicken might seem like a strange choice for breakfast, but many cultures eat poultry in the first meal of the day. This is a popular choice when following a Paleo diet. If you have a hectic day ahead of you, this protein- and carb-packed dish will ensure you have energy to spare all morning. To save time, you can use leftover cooked chicken from dinner the night before instead of sautéing raw poultry.

1 teaspoon coconut oil
1½ pounds boneless, skinless chicken breast, diced
1 pumpkin (about 2 pounds), peeled, seeded, and diced
1 red bell pepper, diced
2 scallions, chopped
1 teaspoon chopped fresh thyme
¼ teaspoon sea salt
¼ teaspoon freshly ground black pepper
2 cups shredded kale

1. In a large skillet over medium-high heat, heat the coconut oil.
2. Sauté the chicken until it is cooked through, about 15 minutes.
3. Add the pumpkin, bell pepper, scallions, thyme, salt, and pepper, and reduce the heat to medium.
4. Sauté, stirring constantly, until the pumpkin breaks down and is heated through, about 10 minutes.
5. Add the kale, and sauté until it is wilted, about 5 minutes.
6. Divide the mixture among 4 bowls, and serve.

Allergy Adjustment: *If poultry is a migraine trigger for you, or you are a vegetarian or vegan, omit the chicken from this recipe. The dish is still delicious.*

PER SERVING Calories: 395; Total Fat: 8g; Saturated Fat: 1g; Cholesterol: 146mg; Total Carbohydrates: 24g; Fiber: 8g; Protein: 59g

Simple Turkey Sausage

Serves 4 / Prep time: 10 minutes / Cook time: 24 minutes

Sausage looks like a difficult product to make, but it is just ground-up meat, spices, and other ingredients such as vegetables or dried fruit. This simple sausage has an assertive herb flavor and very little fat, so it freezes beautifully if you want to make a double batch. Try ground chicken, pork, or a combination of different meats for a different taste. You might love creating interesting sausage combinations so much, that you buy a sausage maker with a simple grinder and casings to make the finished product more traditional looking.

NUT-FREE

1 pound ground turkey
½ cup shredded carrot
1 tablespoon chopped shallot
1 tablespoon chopped fresh parsley
¼ teaspoon sea salt
⅛ teaspoon freshly ground black pepper
Pinch ground cloves
Nonstick olive oil cooking spray

1. In a large bowl, stir together the turkey, carrot, shallot, parsley, salt, pepper, and cloves.

2. Divide the turkey mixture into 8 equal quantities, and form them into half-inch-thick patties.

3. Place a large skillet over medium-high heat, and spray it generously with cooking spray.

4. Cook 4 patties at a time until they are cooked through and golden, about 6 minutes per side, turning once, and then transfer the patties to a paper towel–lined plate.

5. Spray the skillet with cooking spray, and cook the remaining 4 patties.

6. Serve 2 patties per person.

PER SERVING Calories: 229; Total Fat: 13g; Saturated Fat: 2g; Cholesterol: 116mg; Total Carbohydrates: 2g; Fiber: 0g; Protein: 31g

Chapter Seven
Soups and Salads

Shaved Brussels Sprout and Herb Salad

Serves 4 / Prep time: 15 minutes

NUT-FREE

VEGAN

QUICK & EASY

Brussels sprouts are underutilized vegetables that have an undeserved reputation of being unpalatable. Most people find this cruciferous vegetable unpleasant because they have only had it overcooked. When Brussels sprouts are cooked too long, they have a sulfur-like odor that can be off-putting, and the scent can linger long after the vegetables are put away. This salad uses raw Brussels sprouts, so all you will taste is the lovely fresh cabbage flavor. Make sure you wash your shaved Brussels sprouts very well in cold water because grit and dirt can hide in the tight cluster of leaves.

FOR THE SALAD
2 pounds Brussels sprouts
1 scallion, chopped
¼ cup chopped fresh parsley
1 tablespoon chopped fresh cilantro
1 teaspoon chopped fresh thyme

FOR THE VINAIGRETTE
3 tablespoons melted coconut oil
1 tablespoon white vinegar
½ teaspoon grainy mustard
Pinch sea salt
Pinch freshly ground black pepper

TO MAKE THE SALAD

1. Using a vegetable peeler or mandolin, shave the Brussels sprouts into a large bowl.

2. Add the scallion, parsley, cilantro, and thyme. Toss to mix.

TO MAKE THE VINAIGRETTE

1. In a small bowl, whisk the oil, vinegar, mustard, salt, and pepper until blended.

2. Toss the vinaigrette with the Brussels sprout mixture until the vegetables are well coated, and serve.

PER SERVING Calories: 190; Total Fat: 11g; Saturated Fat: 9g; Cholesterol: 0mg; Total Carbohydrates: 21g; Fiber: 9g; Protein: 8g

Green Coleslaw

Serves 4 / Prep time: 25 minutes

Crisp jicama, anise-scented fennel, and lovely, frilly Napa cabbage combine in a pastel mélange that is accented with vibrant green parsley. You can make this coleslaw the night before you need it because the flavors will mellow as it sits.

NUT-FREE

VEGAN

QUICK & EASY

FOR THE DRESSING
¼ cup melted coconut oil
2 tablespoons white vinegar
1 (7g) stevia packet
1 teaspoon ground cumin

FOR THE SLAW
1 small jicama, peeled and shredded
½ small fennel bulb, shredded
¼ head Napa cabbage, cored and shredded
1 scallion, chopped
1 tablespoon chopped fresh parsley
Sea salt
Freshly ground black pepper

TO MAKE THE DRESSING

1. In a small bowl, whisk together the oil, vinegar, stevia, and cumin until well blended.

2. Set aside.

TO MAKE THE SLAW

1. In a large bowl, toss together the jicama, fennel, cabbage, scallions, and parsley.

2. Add the dressing, and stir to coat the vegetables.

3. Season the salad with salt and pepper, and serve.

PER SERVING Calories: 209; Total Fat: 14g; Saturated Fat: 12g; Cholesterol: 0 mg; Total Carbohydrates: 20g; Fiber: 11g; Protein: 3g

Jicama-Melon Salad with Cucumber Dressing

Serves 4 / Prep time: 30 minutes

Salads don't have to be composed of vegetables, even if the dressing is more savory than sweet. The sweet melon is complemented by the lemony taste of coriander in the pale green dressing, as well as the bite of chopped scallion. Watermelon would also make a tasty addition to this pretty salad if you prefer the taste. For a truly sublime dressing, grind your own coriander seeds with a mortar and pestle, or a clean coffee grinder, after toasting them lightly in a skillet over low heat.

NUT-FREE

VEGAN

QUICK & EASY

FOR THE DRESSING

½ English cucumber, cut into chunks

1 (7g) stevia packet

1 teaspoon white vinegar

1 teaspoon ground coriander

FOR THE SALAD

1 small jicama, peeled and shredded

2 cups cantaloupe, finely diced

2 cups honeydew melon, finely diced

1 red bell pepper, diced

2 scallions, sliced thin

Sea salt

Freshly ground black pepper

TO MAKE THE DRESSING

1. In a blender, blend the cucumber, stevia, vinegar, and coriander until smooth.

2. Set aside. ▸

JICAMA-MELON SALAD WITH CUCUMBER DRESSING *continued*

TO MAKE THE SALAD

1. In a large bowl, toss together the jicama, cantaloupe, honeydew, bell pepper, and scallions.

2. Add the dressing to the bowl, and toss to coat the ingredients.

3. Season the salad with salt and pepper, and serve.

Allergy Adjustment: *Nightshades can be a dietary concern for people with autoimmune diseases or certain intolerances. Omit the red bell pepper if you cannot tolerate nightshades.*

PER SERVING Calories: 137; Total Fat: 1g; Saturated Fat: 0g; Cholesterol: 0mg; Total Carbohydrates: 32g; Fiber: 11g; Protein: 3g

Waldorf Salad

Serves 4 / Prep time: 20 minutes

Traditional and simple can be best when considering a large-portion salad on a warm summer day. Waldorf salad is a culinary institution created by the maître d'hôtel of New York's Waldorf Astoria Hotel in 1896. You can find variations of the salad in every city in North America and many countries abroad. This fresher version does not contain walnuts or mayonnaise because they can be migraine triggers, but the chicken breast adds substance and flavor.

NUT-FREE

QUICK & EASY

2 Granny Smith apples, cored and chopped

1 teaspoon white vinegar

6 celery stalks, chopped

2 cups halved green grapes

1 pound cooked boneless, skinless chicken breast, chopped

3 cups shredded kale

1. In a large bowl, mix the apples and vinegar until the apple chunks are well coated.

2. Stir in the celery, grapes, chicken, and kale.

3. Toss the salad to mix the ingredients, and serve.

How It Helps: *Celery contains abundant quantities of a flavonoid called luteolin, which can decrease inflammation in the brain. Celery is also very high in water, which can combat the dehydration that can cause migraines.*

PER SERVING Calories: 315; Total Fat: 4g; Saturated Fat: 0g; Cholesterol: 97mg; Total Carbohydrates: 32g; Fiber: 4g; Protein: 39g

Melon Gazpacho with Basil

Serves 4 / Prep time: 15 minutes

Elegant, pastel pink, and bursting with fresh flavors, this soup is the perfect addition to a special brunch or even as a starter course for a bridal or baby shower. Make this soup the day before so that the flavors have time to mature, and pour it out into special bowls garnished with flowering herbs if you have them in your garden. Flowers from chives, lavender, thyme, and oregano plants would accent the soup beautifully. Look for organic or homegrown herbs because they are not contaminated with pesticides, which can be migraine triggers.

NUT-FREE

VEGAN

QUICK &
EASY

4 cups diced watermelon

1 cup diced cantaloupe

½ English cucumber, peeled and diced

1 red bell pepper, chopped

1 scallion, white and green parts, chopped

¼ cup chopped fresh basil

1 tablespoon chopped fresh parsley

Sea salt

Freshly ground black pepper

Basil leaves, for garnish

1. In a food processor or blender, pulse the watermelon, cantaloupe, cucumber, bell pepper, scallion, basil, and parsley until it reaches the consistency of a thick soup.

2. Season the soup with salt and pepper, and chill in the refrigerator in a sealed container until you wish to serve it.

3. Serve topped with basil leaves.

PER SERVING Calories: 76; Total Fat: 0g; Saturated Fat: 0g; Cholesterol: 0mg; Total Carbohydrates: 18g; Fiber: 2g; Protein: 2g

Kale and Herb Soup

Serves 4 / Prep time: 15 minutes / Cook time: 20 minutes

In areas of the world that have a high-magnesium diet, migraines are relatively rare. Magnesium-rich foods can help reduce the frequency of migraine attacks, so the Swiss chard and kale in this soup are perfect choices. Spinach and watercress would also provide the required minerals and flavor. These dark leafy greens are rich in magnesium and calcium, which is also an important mineral for migraine relief.

NUT-FREE

1 tablespoon coconut oil
½ cup chopped leeks
5 ounces kale, washed and chopped
5 ounces Swiss chard, washed and chopped
4¼ cups Simple Chicken Stock, divided (page 199)
1 teaspoon chopped fresh thyme
1 teaspoon chopped fresh basil
½ teaspoon chopped fresh oregano
2 tablespoons arrowroot powder
½ cup heavy (whipping) cream, optional
Sea salt
Freshly ground black pepper

1. In a large stockpot over medium-high heat, heat the coconut oil.

2. Sauté the leeks until tender, about 4 minutes.

3. Add the kale, Swiss chard, and 4 cups of Simple Chicken Stock, and bring to a boil.

4. Reduce the heat to low, and simmer the soup until the greens are tender, about 10 minutes.

5. Stir in the thyme, basil, and oregano, and simmer for 2 minutes more. ▸

6. Transfer the soup to a blender or use an immersion blender to purée the soup until it is very smooth.

7. Return the soup to the pot.

8. In a small bowl, whisk together the remaining ¼ cup of chicken stock and the arrowroot until smooth.

9. Pour the mixture into the soup, and whisk to blend thoroughly.

10. Bring the soup to a simmer over medium heat until thickened, about 3 minutes.

11. Whisk in the cream, if using, season with salt and pepper, and serve.

PER SERVING Calories: 126; Total Fat: 10g; Saturated Fat: 7g; Cholesterol: 21mg; Total Carbohydrates: 9g; Fiber: 2g; Protein: 3g

Broccoli and Rice Soup

Serves 4 / Prep time: 20 minutes / Cook time: 20 minutes

Some soups are meant to be eaten bundled under a fleece blanket with lots of crusty bread to dip into the flavorful broth. The rice in this fragrant soup adds a hearty thickness that eliminates the need for meat or cream. Using cooked instead of raw rice reduces the cooking time considerably so you can enjoy this dish quickly. Cooked rice holds well in sealed plastic bags, so you can cook a big batch early in the week to use in other recipes. If you want a vegetarian or vegan version, use a gluten-free vegetable broth instead of chicken stock.

NUT-FREE

1 tablespoon coconut oil

2 celery stalks, chopped

¼ cup chopped shallots

4 cups small broccoli florets

1 potato, peeled and chopped

8 cups Simple Chicken Stock (page 199)

¼ cup chopped fresh parsley

2 teaspoons chopped fresh thyme

Sea salt

Freshly ground black pepper

4 cups shredded spinach

1 cup cooked rice

1. In a large stockpot over medium-high heat, heat the coconut oil.

2. Sauté the celery and shallots until softened, about 3 minutes.

3. Add the broccoli, potato, Simple Chicken Stock, parsley, and thyme to the pot.

4. Bring the soup to a boil; then reduce the heat to low and simmer until the vegetables are tender, about 10 minutes. ▸

5. Transfer the soup to a food processor or blender, purée until smooth, and return the soup to the pot.

6. Place the pot over medium heat, season with salt and pepper, and stir in the spinach and rice.

7. Cook until the spinach is wilted and the rice is heated through, about 4 minutes, and serve.

How It Helps: *Spinach is packed with many migraine-fighting nutrients such as vitamins B₁₂ and D as well as calcium. Include this dark leafy green at least three times per week in your meal plans.*

PER SERVING Calories: 300; Total Fat: 5g; Saturated Fat: 3g; Cholesterol: 0mg; Total Carbohydrates: 56g; Fiber: 5g; Protein: 9g

Leek-Parsnip Soup

Serves 4 / Prep time: 20 minutes / Cook time: 30 minutes

Parsnips look like white carrots with less flamboyant greens, but they have an earthy goodness all their own. Parsnips are related to carrots and parsley but have a sweeter flavor and were used as a sweetener in food before cane sugar became readily available. Parsnips are high in vitamins B, C, E, and K, as well as potassium, magnesium, and manganese. Look for firm vegetables that do not bend, and have no brown or soft spots, to ensure a fresh product.

NUT-FREE

1 tablespoon coconut oil

4 leeks, light green and white parts, chopped and washed

4 parsnips, peeled and cut into chunks

1 potato, peeled and chopped

3 cups Simple Chicken Stock (page 199)

½ cup heavy (whipping) cream

½ teaspoon ground nutmeg

Sea salt

Freshly ground black pepper

1. In a large stockpot over medium-high heat, heat the coconut oil.

2. Sauté the leeks until they are tender, about 3 minutes.

3. Add the parsnip, potato, and Simple Chicken Stock, and bring the soup to a boil.

4. Reduce the heat to low, and simmer the soup until the vegetables are tender, about 25 minutes.

5. Transfer the soup to a food processor or blender, and purée until very smooth.

6. Return the soup to the pot, and whisk in the cream and nutmeg.

7. Season with salt and pepper, and serve.

PER SERVING Calories: 277; Total Fat: 10g; Saturated Fat: 7g; Cholesterol: 21mg; Total Carbohydrates: 45g; Fiber: 9g; Protein: 5g

Chickpea and Kale Soup

Serves 4 / Prep time: 20 minutes / Cook time: 40 minutes

Chickpeas, also known as garbanzo beans, are high in protein, fiber, iron, and phosphorus. This hearty legume is not considered a migraine trigger.

NUT-FREE

1 tablespoon coconut oil

3 scallions, chopped

2 celery stalks, sliced

4 cups Simple Chicken Stock (page 199)

1½ cups chickpeas, rinsed and thoroughly drained

1 carrot, peeled and diced

1 sweet potato, peeled and diced

1 bay leaf

2 teaspoons ground cumin

1 teaspoon ground coriander

2 cups loosely packed shredded kale leaves

Sea salt

Freshly ground black pepper

1. In a large stockpot over medium-high heat, heat the coconut oil.

2. Sauté the scallions and celery until tender, about 4 minutes.

3. Add the Simple Chicken Stock, chickpeas, carrot, sweet potato, bay leaf, cumin, and coriander. Bring the soup to a boil. Reduce the heat to low, and simmer until the vegetables and the chickpeas are tender, 25 to 30 minutes.

4. Take out the bay leaf, and stir in the kale. Simmer until the kale is wilted, about 4 minutes.

5. Season with salt and pepper, and serve.

Allergy Adjustment: *The chicken stock in this colorful soup can be replaced with vegetable stock if you want a vegan or vegetarian dish. Use either home-made stock or a product that does not contain a great deal of additives.*

PER SERVING Calories: 205; Total Fat: 7g; Saturated Fat: 3g; Cholesterol: 0mg; Total Carbohydrates: 28g; Fiber: 6g; Protein: 9g

Chicken-Cabbage Soup

Serves 4 / Prep time: 15 minutes / Cook time: 40 minutes

If you have leftover chicken from Sunday dinner, try this simple soup full of vegetables and fresh herbs. You can even use the poultry carcass to make the stock for your healthy soup if you plan ahead. One carcass should make exactly the right amount of stock for this soup, and it is a healthier option than purchased products. Any vegetables would be lovely, so use up whatever is in your refrigerator, and enjoy.

NUT-FREE

2 tablespoons coconut oil
2 leeks, white and light green parts, chopped and washed
1 celery stalk, chopped
4 cups shredded green cabbage
2 carrots, cut into disks
8 cups Simple Chicken Stock (page 199)
2 bay leaves
2 cups chopped cooked chicken
2 teaspoons chopped fresh thyme
Sea salt
Freshly ground black pepper

1. In a large saucepan over medium-high heat, heat the coconut oil.

2. Sauté the leeks and celery until the vegetables are tender, about 3 minutes.

3. Add the cabbage, carrots, Simple Chicken Stock, and bay leaves, and bring the soup to a boil.

4. Reduce the heat to low, and simmer until the vegetables are tender, about 25 minutes.

5. Add the chicken and thyme, and simmer until the chicken is heated through, about 5 minutes.

6. Remove the bay leaves, season with salt and pepper, and serve.

PER SERVING Calories: 243; Total Fat: 10g; Saturated Fat: 7g; Cholesterol: 54mg; Total Carbohydrates: 15g; Fiber: 4g; Protein: 24g

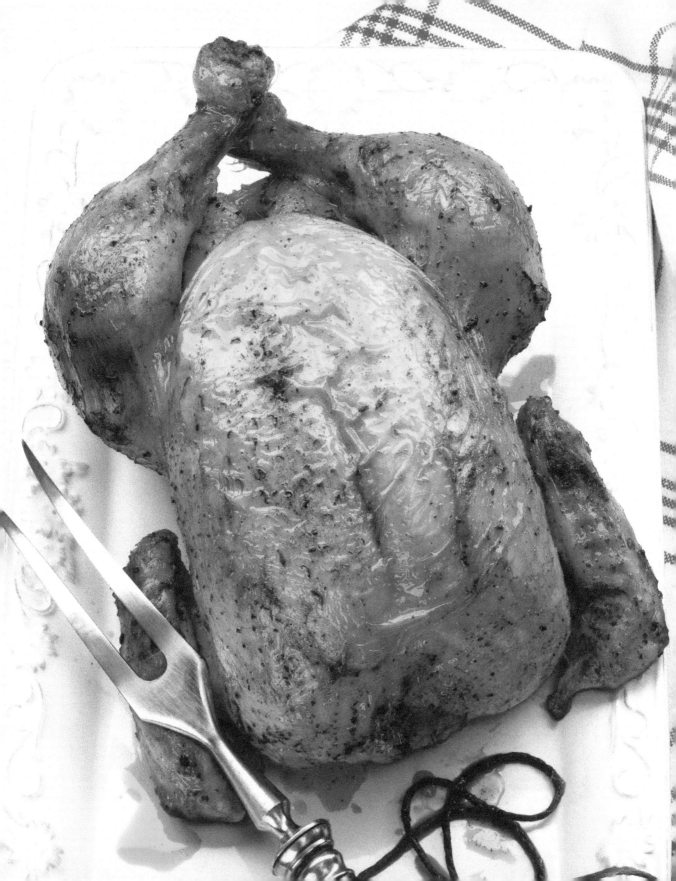

Chapter Eight

Mains: Meat, Poultry, and Seafood

Roasted Halibut with Bell Pepper Salsa

Serves 4 / Prep time: 25 minutes / Cook time: 15 minutes

NUT-FREE

Cold-water fish such as halibut are very high in omega-3 fatty acids, which reduce migraine-causing inflammation and help keep blood vessels from constricting. Choose firm fish with very little fishy odor and bright scales if the skin is still on the fillets. When you press the fish lightly with your fingertips, there should be very little give in the flesh. Always ask to examine your fish purchases closely before letting the fishmonger wrap them up.

FOR THE SALSA

1 red bell pepper, halved and seeded
1 orange bell pepper, halved and seeded
1 tablespoon melted coconut oil
½ English cucumber, peeled and chopped
½ mango, peeled, pitted, and chopped
1 tablespoon white vinegar
1 teaspoon chopped fresh basil
1 teaspoon chopped fresh oregano

FOR THE FISH

4 (6-ounce) halibut fillets
1 tablespoon coconut oil, melted
Sea salt
Freshly ground black pepper

TO MAKE THE SALSA

1. Preheat the oven to broil.

2. In a small stainless steel bowl, toss the red and orange bell pepper halves with the oil. Transfer the peppers to a baking sheet.

3. Broil the peppers until they are lightly charred and tender, turning once, about 6 minutes total.

4. Remove the peppers from the oven and return them to the bowl. Cover the bowl tightly with plastic wrap, and set aside for 10 minutes to steam.

5. Take the peppers out of the bowl, and peel the skin off. Chop the peppers, and transfer them to a small bowl.

6. Add the cucumber, mango, vinegar, basil, and oregano, and stir to mix.

7. Set aside.

TO MAKE THE FISH

1. Reduce the oven heat to 350°F.

2. Line a small baking sheet with foil.

3. Place the fish fillets on the sheet, and drizzle them with the coconut oil.

4. Season the fish lightly with salt and pepper, and bake until the fish is opaque, turning once, about 5 minutes per side or until fish flakes easily with a fork.

5. Spoon the salsa on top of the fish, and serve.

PER SERVING Calories: 256; Total Fat: 8g; Saturated Fat: 6g; Cholesterol: 30mg; Total Carbohydrates: 14g; Fiber: 3g; Protein: 31g

Old-Fashioned "Battered" Fish

Serves 4 / Prep time: 20 minutes / Cook time: 10 minutes

If you are expecting a thick coating of English-style batter, this light crispy coating will be a surprise. The variety of spices in the flour coating adds a pleasing heat, and accents the mild flesh of the haddock well. Other firm white-fleshed fish can be used in this recipe, such as halibut or cod, if you prefer their flavor. If you want a little extra kick, a pinch of cloves, coriander, or allspice would round out the flavor profile of this simple dish.

16 ounces boneless, skinless haddock fillet, cut into 4 equal pieces
½ cup rice flour
¼ teaspoon ground paprika
Pinch ground nutmeg
Pinch red pepper flakes
Pinch ground cinnamon
Pinch ground cardamom
Pinch sea salt
Pinch freshly ground black pepper
¼ cup heavy (whipping) cream
2 tablespoons coconut oil

1. Rinse the fish in cold water, and pat them completely dry with paper towels.

2. In a small bowl, whisk together the rice flour, paprika, nutmeg, red pepper flakes, cinnamon, cardamom, salt, and pepper until well blended.

3. Pour the cream into another small bowl, and set it beside the flour mixture.

4. Dredge a fish fillet in the flour mixture, shaking off any extra.

5. Dip the fillet into the cream, shaking off the excess liquid.

NUT-FREE

QUICK & EASY

6. Dredge the fish in the flour again to coat completely, and set aside.

7. Repeat with the remaining fish fillets.

8. In a large skillet over medium-high heat, heat the coconut oil.

9. When the oil is hot, place the fish fillets in the skillet, and fry until the fish is golden and crispy, about 5 minutes.

10. Using a spatula, flip the fish over and cook the other side until it is golden and the fish is completely cooked through, about 5 minutes.

11. Serve.

Allergy Adjustments: *If capsicum is one of your migraine triggers, exclude the red pepper flakes. Even a pinch of the spice can be an issue.*

PER SERVING Calories: 273; Total Fat: 12g; Saturated Fat: 10g; Cholesterol: 20mg; Total Carbohydrates: 16g; Fiber: 1g; Protein: 22g

Baked Tilapia with Bok Choy and Spinach

Serves 4 / Prep time: 20 minutes / Cook time: 20 minutes

Fish baked in packets of foil or parchment preserve every drop of flavorful juice. The vegetable bed under the fillets gives you a ready-made side dish of steamed spinach and bok choy to accompany the meal. Thinly sliced carrots or shredded sweet potato can be added to create a more colorful meal.

NUT-FREE

2 cups shredded bok choy, divided
2 cups chopped spinach, divided
2 scallions, chopped, divided
2 teaspoons chopped fresh thyme, divided
4 (8-ounce) boneless tilapia fillets
Sea salt
Freshly ground black pepper
4 teaspoons water, divided
2 teaspoons coconut oil, melted, divided

1. Preheat the oven to 400°F.

2. Lay out 4 sheets of aluminum foil about 12 inches long.

3. Place ½ cup each of bok choy and spinach, a quarter of the scallions, and ½ teaspoon thyme thyme in the middle of each sheet of foil.

4. Place a fish fillet on each vegetable pile, and season the fish with salt and pepper.

5. Drizzle the fish and vegetables in each packet with 1 teaspoon of water and ½ teaspoon of coconut oil, and fold the foil up to form loose packets.

6. Set the packets on a baking sheet, and bake until the fish is opaque, about 20 minutes.

7. Open the packets carefully, and serve.

PER SERVING Calories: 283; Total Fat: 11g; Saturated Fat: 5g; Cholesterol: 113mg; Total Carbohydrates: 3g; Fiber: 2g; Protein: 44g

Salmon with Creamy Leek Sauce

Serves 4 / Prep time: 15 minutes / Cook time: 20 minutes

NUT-FREE

Salmon is a popular choice for most home cooks because it is easy to prepare and relatively inexpensive, as long as you don't buy line-caught king salmon. Look for wild-caught Pacific salmon from Canada or Alaska to avoid mercury contamination and radiation issues. The firm flesh of salmon benefits from gentle poaching in this creamy, herb-infused sauce. Use tongs to completely immerse the salmon slices in the sauce to ensure even cooking; you don't want parts of the fish sticking out above the sauce.

1 tablespoon coconut oil
4 leeks, white and light green parts, thinly sliced
½ cup Simple Chicken Stock (page 199)
1 cup heavy (whipping) cream
1½ pounds salmon fillet, cut widthwise into 1-inch-wide pieces
1 teaspoon chopped fresh thyme
Sea salt
Freshly ground black pepper

1. In a large skillet over medium-high heat, heat the coconut oil.

2. Add the leeks, and sauté until they are tender, about 5 minutes.

3. Add the Simple Chicken Stock and cream, and bring the mixture to a boil.

4. Add the salmon pieces to the liquid in a single layer, and reduce the heat to medium-low. Simmer until the salmon is just cooked through, about 7 minutes.

5. Divide the salmon pieces among 4 plates, and stir the thyme into the leek-cream sauce.

6. Season the sauce with salt and pepper, spoon it over the salmon, and serve.

PER SERVING Calories: 414; Total Fat: 25g; Saturated Fat: 11g; Cholesterol: 16mg; Total Carbohydrates: 14g; Fiber: 2g; Protein: 45g

Jambalaya

Serves 6 / Prep time: 20 minutes / Cook time: 1 hour, 5 minutes

Jambalaya is a humble dish designed to use up ingredients in the refrigerator and leftovers in some cases. The presentation can be a little messy because of the hodgepodge of meats, fish, spices, and vegetables. You might be reminded of paella when sampling this popular Cajun dish, even without the tomato base and hot spices. Chopped fish and pork would also be tasty additions to this hearty meal.

1 tablespoon coconut oil
1 pound boneless, skinless chicken breast, cut into strips
Sea salt
Freshly ground black pepper
2 leeks, white and light green parts, washed and chopped
1 red bell pepper, chopped
1 yellow bell pepper, chopped
2 cups white rice
3 cups Simple Chicken Stock (page 199)
Splash Tabasco hot sauce
6 large (16 to 20 count) shrimp, peeled, deveined, and chopped
¼ teaspoon ground cayenne pepper
1 scallion, chopped, for garnish

1. Preheat the oven to 350°F.
2. In a large ovenproof skillet over medium-high heat, heat the coconut oil.
3. Season the chicken lightly with salt and pepper, and sauté in the oil until just cooked through, about 6 minutes.
4. Using a slotted spoon, remove the chicken to a small bowl.
5. Add the leeks and red and yellow bell peppers to the skillet, and sauté until tender, about 4 minutes.

NUT-FREE

6. Return the chicken breast to the skillet, and stir to combine with the vegetables.

7. Stir in the rice, Simple Chicken Stock, hot sauce, shrimp, and cayenne pepper.

8. Bring the mixture to a boil, cover the skillet, and place it in the oven for 40 minutes, stirring occasionally.

9. Remove the cover, and bake until the rice is tender and most of the liquid is absorbed, about 15 minutes.

10. Garnish with the scallion, and serve.

Allergy Adjustment: *Exclude the shrimp if you have a seafood allergy. This is one of the most dangerous allergies, as even a touch of shellfish can be deadly.*

PER SERVING Calories: 430; Total Fat: 9g; Saturated Fat: 4g; Cholesterol: 79mg; Total Carbohydrates: 56g; Fiber: 2g; Protein: 29g

Ginger-Chicken Wraps

Serves 4 / Prep time: 15 minutes

Ginger is a centuries-old medicinal ingredient used for digestive issues and detoxing the body. Ginger can help alleviate nausea, boost immunity, relieve pain associated with osteoarthritis, and reduce the risk of cancer. Ginger is an excellent source of vitamins B_6 and C, magnesium, potassium, manganese, and copper. This rhizome adds a pleasing heat to any dish, so if you like spicy food, increase the amount of grated ginger. Look for firm, unblemished ginger roots with no wizened areas or moldy spots for the best quality.

1 pound cooked boneless, skinless chicken breast, chopped

1 cup shredded fennel

1 cup shredded English cucumber, liquid squeezed out

½ cup shredded carrot

½ cup shredded jicama

1 scallion, chopped

1 teaspoon chopped fresh cilantro

½ teaspoon grated fresh ginger

Pinch sea salt

8 Boston lettuce leaves

1. In a large bowl, toss together the chicken, fennel, cucumber, carrot, jicama, scallion, cilantro, ginger, and salt until well combined.

2. Divide the chicken salad evenly among the lettuce leaves.

3. Wrap the leaves around the filling by folding over two opposite sides and then rolling the leaves into cylinders.

4. Serve.

PER SERVING Calories: 212; Total Fat: 4g; Saturated Fat: 0g; Cholesterol: 97mg; Total Carbohydrates: 6g; Fiber: 2g; Protein: 37g

NUT-FREE

QUICK & EASY

Chicken Shepherd's Pie

Serves 6 / Prep time: 20 minutes / Cook time: 55 minutes

Some potatoes are better than others for mashing, as you might have discovered when you ended up with a gluey mess from using medium- to low-starch potatoes. High-starch potatoes, such as russets, soak up lots of liquid and separate when cooked, creating a perfect fluffy texture. If you can't find russets in your local store, try baking potatoes rather than white or Yukon Gold. Sweet potatoes can be mashed smooth and fluffy for an interesting variation.

NUT-FREE

3 large russet potatoes, peeled and cut into 1-inch chunks

¼ cup heavy (whipping) cream

Sea salt

Freshly ground black pepper

2 teaspoons coconut oil

1 pound boneless, skinless chicken breast, cut into ½-inch chunks

2 shallots, chopped

½ zucchini, diced

2 carrots, peeled, cut into thin disks, and blanched

2¼ cups Simple Chicken Stock (page 199), divided

2 tablespoons arrowroot powder

1 teaspoon chopped fresh thyme

1. Preheat the oven to 325°F.

2. In a large saucepan over high heat, cover the potatoes in enough cold water to cover them by 2 inches.

3. Bring the potatoes to a boil. Reduce the heat to low, and simmer until the potatoes are fork tender, about 20 minutes.

4. Drain the potatoes, and using a fork or potato masher, mash them with the cream until fluffy.

5. Season with salt and pepper, and set aside. ▸

6. In a large skillet over medium-high heat, heat the coconut oil.

7. Sauté the chicken breast until just cooked through, about 10 minutes.

8. Add the shallots and zucchini, and sauté an additional 5 minutes.

9. Stir in the carrots and 2 cups of Simple Chicken Stock.

10. In a small bowl, whisk together the remaining chicken stock and the arrowroot until smooth; set aside.

11. Bring the chicken mixture to a boil, and whisk in the arrowroot mixture.

12. Stir, simmering, until the stock thickens, about 4 minutes.

13. Remove the mixture from the heat, stir in the thyme, and season with salt and pepper.

14. Transfer the chicken mixture to a 9-by-13-inch baking dish, and top it evenly with the mashed potato.

15. Bake until the potatoes are lightly browned and the filling is bubbly, about 15 minutes, and serve.

PER SERVING Calories: 317; Total Fat: 8g; Saturated Fat: 4g; Cholesterol: 78mg; Total Carbohydrates: 33g; Fiber: 5g; Protein: 28g

Chicken-Broccoli Casserole

Serves 4 / Prep time: 15 minutes / Cook time: 35 minutes

Many nutrition professionals consider broccoli a superfood, and this cruciferous vegetable is more effective at lowering cholesterol when it has been lightly blanched, like in this recipe. Broccoli is also a powerful choice for detoxification and reducing inflammation in the body. It is extremely high in vitamins K and C as well as chromium, fiber, and phosphorous. Look for tight florets with no yellowing and stalks that are not split or dried.

NUT-FREE

1 tablespoon coconut oil

2 tablespoons arrowroot powder

1 cup unsweetened rice milk

1 teaspoon chopped fresh thyme

¼ teaspoon ground nutmeg

Sea salt

Freshly ground black pepper

1 pound cooked chicken breast, diced

3 cups cooked white rice

1 head broccoli, cut into small florets and blanched

1. Preheat the oven to 350°F.

2. In a small saucepan over medium-high heat, heat the coconut oil.

3. Whisk the arrowroot into the oil until a paste forms. Whisk the rice milk into the mixture until the sauce is thickened, about 3 minutes.

4. Remove the sauce from the heat, and whisk in the thyme and nutmeg. Season the sauce with salt and pepper.

5. In a large bowl, toss together the chicken, rice, and broccoli. Pour the sauce into the chicken mixture, and stir to coat.

6. Transfer the mixture to a 9-by-9-inch baking dish. Bake the casserole until it is warmed through, about 30 minutes, and serve.

PER SERVING Calories: 515; Total Fat: 9g; Saturated Fat: 3g; Cholesterol: 97mg; Total Carbohydrates: 65g; Fiber: 5g; Protein: 44g

Golden Roast Chicken

Serves 6 / Prep time: 10 minutes, plus 15 minutes resting /
Cook time: 1 hour, 30 minutes

NUT-FREE

Roast chicken is a culinary triumph that looks like you spent hours slaving in the kitchen, when the preparation really takes about 10 minutes. The type of herb you use in the chicken cavity to provide flavor is entirely up to your own personal preference and what you might have available in the refrigerator or garden. Sage, savory, and marjoram are all lovely alternatives to the thyme and rosemary in this recipe. Lemon or orange quarters, ginger, and lavender also make interesting and fragrant stuffing options for the roasted bird.

1 (4-pound) whole roasting chicken
1 teaspoon sea salt, divided
4 shallots, peeled and lightly crushed
4 sprigs fresh thyme
2 sprigs fresh rosemary
1 tablespoon coconut oil, melted
¼ teaspoon freshly ground black pepper

1. Preheat the oven to 350°F.
2. Wash the chicken in cold water, inside and out, and pat it completely dry with paper towels.
3. Place the chicken in a baking dish, and lightly salt the cavity with ½ teaspoon of salt.
4. Place the shallots, thyme, and rosemary in the cavity.
5. Brush the chicken skin all over with the coconut oil, and season the skin with the remaining ½ teaspoon of salt, and the pepper.
6. Roast the chicken until it is golden brown and cooked through (internal temperature of 185°F), about 1 hour and 30 minutes.
7. Remove the chicken from the oven, and let it sit for 15 minutes before removing the shallots, thyme, and rosemary from the cavity.
8. Carve the chicken, and serve.

PER SERVING Calories: 174; Total Fat: 6g; Saturated Fat: 1g; Cholesterol: 25mg;
Total Carbohydrates: 3g; Fiber: 0g; Protein: 25g

Turkey Quinoa Pilaf

Serves 4 / Prep time: 15 minutes / Cook time: 15 minutes

Quinoa has a mild, pleasing taste and is considered a complete protein, containing all 9 essential amino acids. Quinoa is also an excellent source of calcium and iron, so eating this tiny grain supports a healthy cardiovascular system.

○
NUT-FREE

○
QUICK &
EASY

1 tablespoon coconut oil

1 leek, white and light green parts, chopped

1 red bell pepper, diced

1 zucchini, diced

1 carrot, diced and blanched until tender

2 cups chopped cooked turkey

4 cups cooked quinoa

½ cup chopped fresh parsley

½ teaspoon chopped fresh thyme

Sea salt

Freshly ground black pepper

1. In a large skillet over medium-high heat, heat the coconut oil.

2. Sauté the leek, bell pepper, zucchini, and carrot until tender, about 6 minutes.

3. Add the turkey, and sauté until hot, about 4 minutes.

4. Stir in the quinoa, parsley, and thyme, and sauté until well combined and warmed through, about 5 minutes.

5. Season the pilaf with salt and pepper, and serve.

How It Helps: *Quinoa is coated with saponins, a compound that has a bitter, soapy taste, so it is important to rinse the quinoa thoroughly before cooking it. Some people are sensitive to saponins—especially those with autoimmune diseases.*

PER SERVING Calories: 501; Total Fat: 12g; Saturated Fat: 5g; Cholesterol: 53mg; Total Carbohydrates: 63g; Fiber: 8g; Protein: 34g

Grilled Lamb Chops with Mint Pesto

Serves 4 / Prep time: 15 minutes, plus 30 minutes resting /
Cook time: 6 minutes

NUT-FREE

Lamb is not considered a common ingredient in North American kitchens, although it is a staple meat in Northern Africa, New Zealand, and Australia. These more arid regions don't support cattle ranching, but sheep and lambs flourish. Quality North American lamb is helping this delicious protein choice gain popularity in everyday home cooking. Grilled lamb needs very little spice or accompanying ingredients to create a spectacular-tasting dish, so this recipe pairs the tender protein with traditional mint.

FOR THE PESTO
½ cup fresh mint
¼ cup fresh basil
2 tablespoons chopped fresh parsley
3 tablespoons coconut oil
1 tablespoon white vinegar
Pinch red pepper flakes

FOR THE LAMB CHOPS
8 lamb loin chops about 1 inch thick
1 tablespoon coconut oil
Sea salt
Freshly ground black pepper

TO MAKE THE PESTO

1. In a blender, pulse the mint, basil, parsley, oil, vinegar, and red pepper flakes until puréed.

2. Transfer the pesto to a small bowl. Set aside.

TO MAKE THE LAMB CHOPS

1. Rub the lamb chops with the coconut oil, and season them lightly with salt and pepper. Set the chops aside at room temperature for 30 minutes before grilling them. Preheat the barbecue or a grill pan on the stove to medium-high heat.

2. Grill the lamb until desired doneness, turning once, about 3 minutes per side for medium-rare.

3. Let the lamb rest for 10 minutes, and serve topped with the mint pesto.

How It Helps: *This recipe packs a hefty amount of mint in the sauce that accompanies the grilled lamb. Mint has been proven to be very effective for helping prevent migraines through the lovely scent of the herb and the essential oils that are released when you purée the leaves.*

PER SERVING Calories: 441; Total Fat: 26g; Saturated Fat: 16g; Cholesterol: 153mg; Total Carbohydrates: 1g; Fiber: 1g; Protein: 48g

Beef Vegetable Stew

Serves 6 / Prep time: 20 minutes / Cook time: 1 hour, 40 minutes

NUT-FREE

Traditional meals are often the first culinary casualties when you are trying to follow a diet that addresses a health concern such as migraine headaches, so it is nice to know that hearty, comforting beef stew is still a meal to enjoy. Some people who experience migraines are sensitive to beef, so swap it out for chicken if you have problems with red meat. The other ingredients will combine beautifully with whatever protein you use in the dish.

1 tablespoon coconut oil
1 pound beef chuck roast, cut into ½-inch chunks
3 shallots, chopped
2 celery stalks, diced
5 cups Dark Beef Stock (page 200)
2 carrots, peeled and diced
2 parsnips, peeled and diced
1 potato, peeled and diced
1 cup shredded green cabbage
1 tablespoon chopped fresh thyme
2 tablespoons water
1 tablespoon arrowroot powder
Sea salt
Freshly ground black pepper

1. In a large stockpot over medium-high heat, heat the coconut oil.

2. Brown the beef chunks on all sides for about 5 minutes.

3. Add the shallots and celery, and sauté for another 3 minutes.

4. Stir in the Dark Beef Stock, and bring the liquid to a boil.

5. Reduce the heat to low, and simmer the beef for 1 hour.

6. Add the carrots, parsnips, and potato, and simmer until the vegetables are tender, about 15 minutes.

7. Stir in the cabbage and thyme, and simmer for an additional 10 minutes.

8. In a small bowl, whisk together the water and arrowroot until blended.

9. Stir the arrowroot mixture into the stew, and stir until the stock is thickened, about 4 minutes.

10. Season the stew with salt and pepper, and serve.

PER SERVING Calories: 381; Total Fat: 24g; Saturated Fat: 11g; Cholesterol: 78mg; Total Carbohydrates: 17g; Fiber: 4g; Protein: 24g

Juicy Meatloaf

Serves 6 / Prep time: 15 minutes / Cook time: 1 hour

This does not taste like a simple meatloaf with only 5 ingredients and a little salt and pepper. The horseradish adds a lovely kick and the apple, a hint of sweetness. Instead of buying a jar of prepared horseradish, grate your own from a fresh piece. Store any unused horseradish in the refrigerator in a sealed bag, or grate the entire root and freeze the pulp in ice cube trays.

2 pounds lean ground beef

1 cup gluten-free breadcrumbs

½ cup chopped shallots

½ cup peeled, cored, and grated Granny Smith apple

1 teaspoon grated horseradish

1 teaspoon sea salt

¼ teaspoon freshly ground black pepper

1. Preheat the oven to 350°F.
2. In a large bowl, mix together the ground beef, breadcrumbs, shallots, apple, horseradish, salt, and pepper until very well combined.
3. Pack the meat mixture into a 9-by-4-inch loaf pan, and bake until cooked through and browned, about 1 hour.
4. Let the meatloaf sit for 10 minutes. Pour off any accumulated grease, and serve.

Allergy Adjustment: *Beef is a migraine trigger for a small percentage of those who suffer from this ailment. If you cannot eat beef, swap out the ground meat for ground chicken in this recipe and exchange the horseradish with grated fresh ginger.*

PER SERVING Calories: 314; Total Fat: 10g; Saturated Fat: 4g; Cholesterol: 135mg; Total Carbohydrates: 8g; Fiber: 0g; Protein: 49g

Beef Fajitas

Serves 4 / Prep time: 20 minutes, plus 2 hours to marinate /
Cook time: 20 minutes

Sweet bell peppers are a main component in fajitas because their sweetness is a perfect foil for the spices in the meat. Try to use at least two colors of peppers because the various colors offer different phytonutrients. Bell peppers are high in vitamins A, B, C, and E as well as calcium, zinc, manganese, and phosphorus. B vitamins have been linked to reducing the frequency and severity of migraines. These pretty vegetables can also help lower cholesterol, boost the immune system, and reduce the risk of digestive issues, cancer, and heart disease.

NUT-FREE

FOR THE MARINADE
4 tablespoons coconut oil, melted, divided
1 tablespoon white vinegar
1 teaspoon ground cumin
¼ teaspoon ground cayenne pepper
Pinch sea salt
Pinch freshly ground black pepper

FOR THE FAJITAS
1 pound flank steak
2 shallots, sliced
1 red bell pepper, cut into thin strips
1 green bell pepper, cut into thin strips
2 tablespoons chopped fresh cilantro
4 gluten-free tortillas

TO MAKE THE MARINADE

1. In a large resealable bag, shake to combine 3 tablespoons of coconut oil with the vinegar, cumin, cayenne, salt, and pepper.

2. Pierce the steak all over with a fork, and place it in the bag with the marinade. ▸

3. Squeeze out as much air as possible, and seal the bag.

4. Marinate the steak for 2 hours in the refrigerator, turning the bag over once.

TO MAKE THE FAJITAS

1. Preheat the barbecue or a grill pan on the stove to medium-high.

2. Grill the steak until medium-rare, turning once, about 5 minutes per side.

3. Remove the steak from the heat, and set aside for 10 minutes.

4. While the meat is resting, in a large skillet over medium-high heat, heat the remaining 1 tablespoon of coconut oil.

5. Sauté the shallots and red and green bell peppers until they are tender and lightly caramelized, about 6 minutes.

6. Remove the vegetables from the heat, and stir in the cilantro.

7. Slice the steak thinly on a bias across the grain, and serve the meat in the tortillas topped with the vegetable mixture.

PER SERVING Calories: 481; Total Fat: 24g; Saturated Fat: 16g; Cholesterol: 62mg; Total Carbohydrates: 29g; Fiber: 3g; Protein: 32g

Beef Brisket with Fall Vegetables

Serves 4 / Prep time: 15 minutes / Cook time: 4 hours, 15 minutes

Brisket is a beef cut that needs careful, moist cooking because this meat has a great deal of connective tissue. If your brisket has a fat cap, leave it on for the cooking process so that the meat stays moist. You can always cut the cap off after the meat is tender and cooked through.

NUT-FREE

1 tablespoon coconut oil

1 pound beef brisket

½ teaspoon sea salt

½ teaspoon freshly ground black pepper

4 shallots, cut into eighths

3 carrots, peeled and cut into 1-inch chunks

3 parsnips, peeled and cut into 1-inch chunks

12 new potatoes, washed

3 cups Dark Beef Stock (page 200)

1. In a large stockpot over medium-high heat, heat the coconut oil.

2. Season the brisket with salt and pepper, and brown the beef on both sides in the oil, about 10 minutes total. Remove the meat to a plate.

3. Place the shallots, carrots, parsnips, and potatoes in the stockpot, and put the beef back on top of the vegetables.

4. Pour in the Dark Beef Stock, and bring the liquid to a boil. Reduce the heat to low, and cover the pot.

5. Simmer until the beef is very tender, about 4 hours.

6. Serve the brisket with the vegetables and broth from the pot.

How It Helps: *Potatoes are a fabulous source of potassium, which helps prevent migraines: A medium baked potato has over 900 mg.*

PER SERVING Calories: 464; Total Fat: 11g; Saturated Fat: 6g; Cholesterol: 101mg; Total Carbohydrates: 50g; Fiber: 10g; Protein: 41g

Chapter Nine
Mains: Vegetarian

Salad Rolls with Mango-Ginger Sauce

Serves 4 / Prep time: 30 minutes

Salad rolls are traditional street food in many Asian countries because the various types of lettuce are inexpensive and when rolled can hold an assortment of delectable fillings. The best lettuce leaves for wraps are flexible large leaves that do not have stiff ribs running through then. You can use romaine lettuce leaves if you carefully trim out the large center rib. Save the ribs to use in smoothies or chopped in salads rather than tossing them in the garbage.

FOR THE SAUCE

1 ripe mango, peeled, pitted, and diced coarsely

1 teaspoon grated fresh ginger

½ teaspoon ground cumin

¼ teaspoon ground coriander

¼ cup water

FOR THE SALAD ROLLS

½ cup bean sprouts

½ cup chopped strawberries

½ cup julienned carrot

½ cup julienned jicama

½ cup julienned English cucumber

¼ cup chopped scallion

2 tablespoons chopped fresh mint

Pinch sea salt

8 Boston lettuce leaves

TO MAKE THE SAUCE

1. In a blender, purée the mango, ginger, cumin, coriander, and water until smooth.

2. Refrigerate the sauce in a sealed container.

TO MAKE THE SALAD ROLLS

1. In a large bowl, toss together the bean sprouts, strawberries, carrot, jicama, cucumber, scallion, mint, and salt until well mixed.

2. Evenly divide the filling among the lettuce leaves, and roll the leaves up like tortilla wraps.

3. Serve the rolls with the dipping sauce.

PER SERVING Calories: 100; Total Fat: 1g; Saturated Fat: 0g; Cholesterol: 0mg; Total Carbohydrates: 15g; Fiber: 2g; Protein: 2g

Quinoa-Stuffed Acorn Squash

Serves 4 / Prep time: 20 minutes / Cook time: 1 hour

Vegetables make delightful edible containers for savory and sweet fillings, and acorn squash are the perfect size for individual servings. Acorn squash is very high in beta-carotene, vitamins A and C, fiber, and copper. This winter squash has a nutty, almost peppery flavor that is the perfect backdrop for creamy ricotta cheese, mild quinoa, and sweet red bell pepper. If you have trouble cutting the squash in half, microwave it for about 30 seconds to soften the vegetable.

Coconut oil, for greasing
2 acorn squash, halved and seeded
2 cups cooked quinoa
1 cup canned chickpeas, drained and rinsed
1 cup shredded kale
1 red bell pepper, chopped
½ cup ricotta cheese
1 scallion, chopped
1 tablespoon chopped fresh cilantro
Sea salt
Freshly ground black pepper

1. Preheat the oven to 350°F.
2. Lightly oil a baking sheet, and place the squash, cut-side down, on the sheet.
3. Bake the squash until it is softened, about 30 minutes.
4. While the squash is baking, in a large bowl, stir together the quinoa, chickpeas, kale, bell pepper, ricotta, scallion, and cilantro.
5. Season the filling with salt and pepper.

6. When the squash is soft, take it out of the oven and, using 2 forks, turn the squash over so that the hollow is up.

7. Scoop out about half of the squash flesh from the four halves, and stir it into the quinoa filling.

8. Spoon the filling back into the squash halves, bake until the filling is warmed through, about 30 minutes, and serve.

How It Helps: *The amount of quinoa per serving in this pretty dish is about 20 percent of the daily recommended value for riboflavin, or vitamin B$_2$. Riboflavin supports a healthy energy metabolism in the brain, which can reduce the frequency of migraines.*

PER SERVING Calories: 277; Total Fat: 7g; Saturated Fat: 2g; Cholesterol: 10 mg; Total Carbohydrates: 65g; Fiber: 10g; Protein: 16g

Vegetable Fried Rice

Serves 4 / Prep time: 20 minutes / Cook time: 20 minutes

NUT-FREE

VEGAN

Turmeric adds a glorious bright color and citrusy, peppery flavor to recipes. This spice, a powerful ingredient in ancient Chinese and Indian medicine, is especially effective for digestive issues. Turmeric is an anti-inflammatory that can help treat irritable bowel syndrome, rheumatoid arthritis, and cystic fibrosis. Curcumin, the chemical compound in turmeric, is also a pain reliever that can reduce the severity of migraines.

2 tablespoons coconut oil
1 leek, white and light green parts, chopped
1 tablespoon grated fresh ginger
1 teaspoon ground cumin
¼ teaspoon turmeric
2 carrots, peeled and finely diced
1 cup chopped broccoli
1 red bell pepper, finely chopped
1 zucchini, diced
3 cups cooked rice
Sea salt
2 tablespoons chopped fresh cilantro, for serving

1. In a large skillet over medium-high heat, heat the coconut oil.
2. Sauté the leek, ginger, cumin, and turmeric until the vegetables are softened, about 4 minutes.
3. Stir in the carrots, broccoli, bell pepper, and zucchini, and sauté for 7 minutes.
4. Stir in the rice and fry, stirring constantly, until the rice is heated through, about 10 minutes.
5. Season the rice with salt, and serve topped with the cilantro.

PER SERVING Calories: 370; Total Fat: 8g; Saturated Fat: 6g; Cholesterol: 0mg; Total Carbohydrates: 68g; Fiber: 4g; Protein: 7g

Asparagus Risotto

Serves 4 / Prep time: 15 minutes / Cook time: 30 minutes

Asparagus is a perishable vegetable, so make this creamy risotto within a couple days of purchasing the vegetable. Asparagus is extremely high in vitamins E and K, copper, and has many anti-inflammatory phytonutrients. It also supports digestive health, helps stabilize blood sugar, and fights cancer.

NUT-FREE

VEGAN

4 cups gluten-free vegetable stock
1 tablespoon coconut oil
1 leek, white and light green parts, finely chopped
1 cup Arborio rice
20 asparagus spears, cut into 1-inch pieces and blanched for 1 minute
Sea salt
Freshly ground black pepper

1. In a medium saucepan over medium-high heat, bring the vegetable stock to a boil. Remove it from the heat, and set aside next to the stove.

2. In a medium saucepan over medium heat, heat the coconut oil. Sauté the leek until it is tender, about 3 minutes.

3. Add the rice, and sauté for 3 minutes.

4. Pour in ½ cup of the hot stock, and stir until the liquid is almost absorbed.

5. Add the hot stock by the ½ cupful, stirring between each addition until the liquid is absorbed, until the rice is al dente.

6. Stir in the blanched asparagus, season with salt and pepper, and serve.

How It Helps: *Asparagus is an excellent source of B$_2$, riboflavin, which has been shown to decrease the incidence of migraines by as much as 50 percent. Add a couple of extra spears per serving to increase your riboflavin levels.*

PER SERVING Calories: 248; Total Fat: 6g; Saturated Fat: 5g; Cholesterol: 0mg; Total Carbohydrates: 48g; Fiber: 4g; Protein: 6g

Vegetable Patties

Serves 4 / Prep time: 20 minutes, plus 1 hour to chill / Cook time: 10 minutes

Vegetable burgers have a terrible reputation as dry, flavorless, and strangely textured, but these simple patties are moist and redolent with fresh herbs. You can make a double batch of patties, cook them, and freeze them for up to 1 month for a quick grab-and-go snack or full meal.

NUT-FREE

VEGETARIAN

1 cup canned chickpeas, drained and rinsed
1 carrot, peeled and cut into chunks
2 tablespoons chopped fresh cilantro
2 tablespoons chopped fresh parsley
1 teaspoon white vinegar
½ teaspoon grated fresh ginger
2 cups cooked sushi rice
½ cup heavy (whipping) cream
Pinch sea salt
2 tablespoons coconut oil

1. In a food processor, pulse together the chickpeas, carrot, cilantro, parsley, vinegar, and ginger until a slightly chunky paste forms.

2. Transfer the mixture to a large bowl, and mix in the sushi rice, cream, and salt. Chill the rice mixture in the refrigerator to firm it up for 1 hour.

3. Form the rice mixture into 8 patties.

4. In a large skillet over medium-high heat, heat the coconut oil. Place the patties in the skillet 4 at a time, gently flattening them with a spatula.

5. Cook the patties for 5 minutes or until the bottom is golden, and flip the patties over. Cook the other side for 5 minutes, and transfer the cooked patties to a paper towel–lined plate. Repeat with the remaining 4 patties, and serve.

PER SERVING Calories: 360; Total Fat: 14g; Saturated Fat: 10g; Cholesterol: 21mg; Total Carbohydrates: 49g; Fiber: 4g; Protein: 8g

Butternut Squash and Chickpea Bowl

Serves 4 / Prep time: 20 minutes / Cook time: 20 minutes

The lovely parsley-like flavor in this filling bowl comes from the celeriac. Celeriac is a strange vegetable. When you cut away the unappealing exterior, you will be left with firm white flesh that smells fresh and earthy. Celeriac, also known as celery root, is very low in calories and high in fiber, vitamin C, phosphorus, and potassium.

NUT-FREE

VEGAN

FOR THE DRESSING

¼ cup melted coconut oil

2 tablespoons white vinegar

1 (7g) stevia packet

¼ teaspoon ground cinnamon

Pinch ground cumin

Sea salt

Freshly ground black pepper

FOR THE SALAD

1 small butternut squash, peeled, seeded, and diced

2 large carrots, peeled and diced

1 celeriac, peeled and diced

1 tablespoon coconut oil

2 cups canned chickpeas, rinsed and drained well

1 red bell pepper, finely chopped

1 scallion, sliced

TO MAKE THE DRESSING

1. In a small bowl, stir together the coconut oil, vinegar, stevia, cinnamon, and cumin until well blended.

2. Season the dressing with salt and pepper, and set aside. ▸

TO MAKE THE SALAD

1. Preheat the oven to 350°F.
2. Line a baking sheet with parchment paper.
3. In a large bowl, toss together the squash, carrots, and celeriac with the coconut oil until well coated.
4. Transfer the vegetables to the baking sheet, and bake until lightly browned and tender, about 20 minutes.
5. Remove the vegetables from the oven, and let them cool for 15 minutes.
6. Transfer the roasted vegetables to a large bowl, and toss them with the chickpeas, bell pepper, and scallion.
7. Add the dressing, toss to combine, and serve.

PER SERVING Calories: 401; Total Fat: 21g; Saturated Fat: 15g; Cholesterol: 0mg; Total Carbohydrates: 45g; Fiber: 10g; Protein: 11g

Stir-Fried Vegetables with Rice

Serves 4 / Prep time: 15 minutes / Cook time: 15 minutes

Stir-frying is one of the quickest and healthiest cooking methods, whether done in a traditional wok or on your stovetop in a favorite skillet. If you want all your vegetables to turn out tender-crisp, stagger the addition of the ingredients so that the vegetables that are more delicate are added last. This method ensures that nothing will get over- or undercooked.

NUT-FREE

VEGAN

QUICK &
EASY

1 tablespoon coconut oil

1 tablespoon chopped fresh ginger

2 cups broccoli florets

1 cup peeled and sliced carrots

1 celery stalk, sliced

1 red bell pepper, cut into thin strips

1 yellow zucchini, sliced

½ cup jicama, sliced into strips

2 scallions, chopped

2 tablespoons chopped fresh cilantro

4 cups cooked white rice

1. In a large skillet over medium-high heat, heat the coconut oil.

2. Sauté the ginger until it is softened, about 2 minutes.

3. Add the broccoli, carrots, and celery, and sauté until tender-crisp, about 5 minutes.

4. Stir in the bell pepper, zucchini, and jicama, and sauté for 4 minutes.

5. Stir in the scallions and cilantro, and serve the vegetables over the cooked rice.

How It Helps: *Ginger root helps with migraines in two ways. This pungent rhizome, the subterranean stem of a plant, is a powerful anti-inflammatory, and ginger helps treat vomiting and nausea.*

PER SERVING Calories: 424; Total Fat: 4g; Saturated Fat: 3g; Cholesterol: 0mg; Total Carbohydrates: 86g; Fiber: 5g; Protein: 9g

Quinoa Tabbouleh

Serves 4 / Prep time: 30 minutes

Quinoa, radishes, and jicama are not classic ingredients of this Lebanese dish, but the final presentation of finely chopped vegetables, grains, and a generous amount of parsley is close enough. Radishes come in many varieties, so you can adjust the heat of the recipe depending on which radish you chop up. Although Daikon and black radishes add a nice bite to this meal, try using bright red vegetables because the little bits of vibrant color are spectacular.

FOR THE DRESSING
¼ cup melted coconut oil
2 tablespoons white vinegar
1 tablespoon minced mint
Pinch sea salt

FOR THE TABBOULEH
3 cups cooked quinoa
4 radishes, finely chopped
2 red bell peppers, finely chopped
1 jicama, peeled and finely chopped
½ English cucumber, finely chopped
½ cup chopped fresh parsley
¼ cup chopped fresh mint

TO MAKE THE DRESSING

1. Whisk together the oil, vinegar, mint, and salt until well combined.
2. Set aside.

TO MAKE THE TABBOULEH

1. Toss together the quinoa, radishes, bell pepper, jicama, cucumber, parsley, and mint in a large bowl until very well mixed.
2. Add the dressing and stir to combine.
3. Serve.

PER SERVING Calories: 447; Total Fat: 18g; Saturated Fat: 12g; Cholesterol: 0mg; Total Carbohydrates: 62g; Fiber: 15g; Protein: 12g

Roasted Spaghetti Squash Casserole

Serves 4 / Prep time: 25 minutes / Cook time: 1 hour

Any white rice works in this recipe, but a firmer-textured choice would be best so that the rice does not fall apart while the casserole bakes. Medium-grain rice such as bomba, a Spanish rice, cooks up tender and soaks up a great deal of liquid without getting sticky. However, since you are stirring the rice into the casserole, using a nutty basmati would be acceptable. Brown rice would also work in the dish due to its chewy texture and its high migraine-busting magnesium content.

NUT-FREE

VEGAN

1 spaghetti squash, halved and seeded
3 teaspoons coconut oil, divided
2 cups cooked white rice
2 celery stalks, chopped
1 carrot, peeled and finely diced
1 parsnip, peeled and finely diced
½ cup shredded spinach
½ cup gluten-free vegetable stock
1 teaspoon chopped fresh thyme
¼ teaspoon sea salt

1. Preheat the oven to 400°F.
2. Rub the cut side of the spaghetti squash with 2 teaspoons of coconut oil, and place the squash cut-side down on a baking sheet.
3. Bake until the squash is soft, about 30 minutes.
4. Remove the squash from the oven, and let it cool for 10 minutes. ▶

5. Scoop the cooked squash strands out, and transfer them to a large bowl.

6. Add the rice, celery, carrot, parsnip, spinach, vegetable stock, thyme, and salt to the squash, and stir to combine.

7. Lightly grease a 9-by-9-inch casserole dish with the remaining 1 teaspoon of coconut oil, and spoon the squash mixture into the dish.

8. Bake until the casserole is warmed through and the vegetables are tender, about 30 minutes, and serve.

PER SERVING Calories: 264; Total Fat: 5g; Saturated Fat: 3g; Cholesterol: 0mg; Total Carbohydrates: 52g; Fiber: 3g; Protein: 5g

Wild Rice Cabbage Tureen

Serves 4 / Prep time: 25 minutes / Cook time: 50 minutes

Wild rice is a grass, not a grain, indigenous to areas of Canada and the United States. This nutritional powerhouse was labeled as rice when English explorers observed Native Americans harvesting the aquatic grass with the same technique Asian women used for rice. Read the label on the wild rice you purchase in the grocery store to authenticate that the product is real wild grown, because many brands are a cultivated version.

NUT-FREE

VEGAN

FOR THE SAUCE
3 tablespoons chopped fresh cilantro

2 tablespoons white vinegar

1 tablespoon coconut oil

1 teaspoon grated fresh ginger

1 (7g) stevia packet

½ teaspoon ground cumin

Pinch ground cloves

FOR THE RICE
2 cups dry wild rice

1 cup shredded green cabbage

1 carrot, peeled and shredded

1 parsnip, peeled and shredded

½ celeriac, peeled and shredded

1 cup chopped Granny Smith apple

2 scallions, sliced thinly on a bias, for serving

TO MAKE THE SAUCE

1. In a blender, pulse the cilantro, vinegar, coconut oil, ginger, stevia, cumin, and cloves until smooth.

2. Set aside. ▸

TO MAKE THE RICE

1. In a large saucepan over medium-high heat, cover the rice by 3 inches with water and bring to a boil.

2. Reduce the heat to low, and simmer until the rice is tender, about 45 minutes.

3. Drain the rice, and transfer it to a large bowl.

4. Add the cabbage, carrot, parsnip, celeriac, and apple to the rice, and toss to mix.

5. Stir the sauce into the rice, and serve the wild rice topped with the scallions.

PER SERVING Calories: 226; Total Fat: 4g; Saturated Fat: 3g; Cholesterol: 0mg; Total Carbohydrates: 43g; Fiber: 6g; Protein: 7g

Classic Colcannon

Serves 4 / Prep time: 10 minutes / Cook time: 25 minutes

A picture of colcannon should be in the dictionary under "comfort food," because this is the meal you will want to eat snuggled under a quilt after a bad day. Fluffy mashed potatoes mixed with tender vegetables provide a substantial rib-sticking dish with lots of flavor. If eating meat does not trigger your migraines, try adding sliced freshly cooked sausage to the mixture before baking it. This dish does not freeze well, so eat any leftovers for lunch the next day.

○ NUT-FREE

○ VEGETARIAN

○ QUICK & EASY

2 tablespoons coconut oil
2 leeks, white and light green parts, chopped
4 cups finely shredded green cabbage
4 cups mashed cooked russet potatoes
½ cup heavy (whipping) cream
½ cup chopped fresh parsley
Sea salt
Freshly ground black pepper

1. In a large skillet over medium-high heat, heat the coconut oil.

2. Sauté the leeks until they are softened, about 4 minutes.

3. Stir in the cabbage, and sauté until the cabbage is tender, about 10 minutes.

4. Stir in the mashed potatoes, cream, and parsley until well mixed.

5. Continue to stir the mixture until it is completely heated through, about 10 minutes.

6. Season the colcannon with salt and pepper, and serve immediately.

Allergy Adjustment: *The heavy cream can be replaced with rice milk if you are lactose intolerant. The texture of the dish might not be as creamy, but the taste will still be spectacular.*

PER SERVING Calories: 268; Total Fat: 15g; Saturated Fat: 9g; Cholesterol: 21mg; Total Carbohydrates: 36g; Fiber: 7g; Protein: 5g

Vegetarian Shepherd's Pie

Serves 6 / Prep time: 20 minutes / Cook time: 1 hour, 10 minutes

NUT-FREE

VEGAN

It should be no surprise that shepherd's pie was traditionally made with minced lamb, and if the dish contained another meat or no meat, it was called a cottage pie. This savory dish originated in Ireland and the United Kingdom, where the poorer members of the populations ate potatoes every day. The mashed potato topping was more inexpensive than a flour crust, and potatoes were a staple ingredient in most households.

3 large russet potatoes, peeled and cut into 2-inch chunks
¼ cup unsweetened rice milk
Sea salt
Freshly ground black pepper
1 tablespoon coconut oil
1 celery stalk, chopped
½ cup chopped shallots
3 carrots, peeled and sliced into disks
2 cups small cauliflower florets
1 zucchini, diced
½ cup gluten-free vegetable broth
1 teaspoon chopped fresh thyme
Pinch red pepper flakes
1 cup canned chickpeas, drained and rinsed

1. In a large saucepan over high heat, cover the potatoes with about 2 inches of cold water.

2. Bring to a boil; then reduce the heat to low and simmer until the potatoes are fork tender, about 20 minutes.

3. Drain the potatoes, and using a fork or potato masher, mash them with rice milk until fluffy.

4. Season the mashed potatoes with salt and pepper, and set aside.

5. Preheat the oven to 350°F.

6. In a large skillet over medium-high heat, heat the coconut oil.

7. Sauté the celery and shallots until tender, about 4 minutes.

8. Add the carrot, cauliflower, and zucchini to the skillet, and sauté for 10 minutes.

9. Stir in the vegetable broth, thyme, and pepper flakes.

10. Bring the mixture to a boil; then reduce the heat to low and simmer until the vegetables are tender.

11. Remove the skillet from the heat, and stir in the chickpeas.

12. Spoon the vegetable mixture into a 9-by-13-inch baking dish, and top evenly with the mashed potatoes.

13. Bake the casserole until it is bubbling and lightly browned, about 35 minutes, and serve.

PER SERVING Calories: 238; Total Fat: 4g; Saturated Fat: 2g; Cholesterol: 0mg; Total Carbohydrates: 45g; Fiber: 8g; Protein: 8g

Cheesy Kale Macaroni

Serves 4 / Prep time: 5 minutes / Cook time: 30 minutes

NUT-FREE

VEGETARIAN

Cream cheese is a mild cheese that is not aged, so it is appropriate for a migraine diet. Aged cheese contains tyramine, which is created when proteins break down. The longer a high-protein food ages, the higher the amount of tyramine, so cheeses such as Cheddar and Parmesan are poor choices if you have migraines. Cream cheese, ricotta, and cottage cheese can all be used with no ill effects. This dish is best eaten immediately because the cheese sauce can get quite thick when refrigerated. You might have to stir in a little more rice milk to thin out the sauce if you are reheating the pasta.

1 teaspoon coconut oil, plus more for greasing
2 shallots, chopped
½ cup unsweetened rice milk
1 cup cream cheese
½ teaspoon freshly ground black pepper
¼ teaspoon sea salt
Pinch ground cayenne pepper
1 cup shredded kale
6 cups cooked gluten-free macaroni

1. Preheat the oven to 375°F.
2. Grease a 9-by-9-inch baking dish with coconut oil; set aside.
3. In a large saucepan over medium-high heat, heat the coconut oil.
4. Sauté the shallots until translucent, about 3 minutes.
5. Whisk in the milk, cream cheese, black pepper, salt, and cayenne pepper until the mixture is smooth and creamy.
6. Stir in the kale and cooked macaroni until the noodles are coated, and transfer the noodle mixture to the baking dish.
7. Bake until the macaroni is bubbly and lightly browned, about 15 minutes, and serve.

PER SERVING Calories: 397; Total Fat: 23g; Saturated Fat: 14g; Cholesterol: 64mg; Total Carbohydrates: 38g; Fiber: 4g; Protein: 10g

Pumpkin Curry

Serves 6 / Prep time: 15 minutes / Cook time: 50 minutes

Fall and early winter are the best times to try this fragrant golden stew because pumpkins will be available at your local grocery store. Don't be afraid to get a larger pumpkin even though you only need 4 cups for this recipe because you can freeze any extra pumpkin. Just peel the vegetable, cut it into cubes, and freeze the cubes spread out on a baking sheet. When the pumpkin is completely frozen, transfer the cubes to a freezer bag and store it for up to 3 months in the freezer.

NUT-FREE

VEGAN

1 tablespoon coconut oil

1 leek, white and light green parts, chopped

2 teaspoons grated fresh ginger

4 cups cubed pumpkin

2 potatoes, peeled and diced

1 parsnip, peeled and diced

2 cups gluten-free vegetable stock

1 tablespoon curry powder

1 teaspoon ground cumin

½ teaspoon ground coriander

1 red bell pepper, seeded and cut into strips

3 tablespoons water

2 tablespoons arrowroot powder

3 tablespoons chopped fresh cilantro

1. In a large skillet over medium-high heat, heat the coconut oil.

2. Sauté the leek until it is tender, about 4 minutes.

3. Add the ginger, and sauté for 1 minute.

4. Stir in the pumpkin, potatoes, parsnip, vegetables stock, curry, cumin, and coriander. ▸

5. Bring the liquid to a boil; then reduce the heat to low and simmer, covered, until the vegetables are tender, about 35 minutes.

6. Add the bell pepper, and simmer for 5 minutes more.

7. In a small bowl, stir together the water and arrowroot.

8. Add the arrowroot mixture to the curry, and stir until the sauce is thickened, about 4 minutes.

9. Stir in the cilantro, and serve.

Allergy Adjustment: *Replace the potatoes with sweet potatoes in this curry if you cannot eat nightshade vegetables. The sweet potatoes will combine nicely with the pumpkin.*

PER SERVING Calories: 132; Total Fat: 4g; Saturated Fat: 3g; Cholesterol: 0mg; Total Carbohydrates: 26g; Fiber: 4g; Protein: 3g

Root Vegetable Stew

Serves 4 / Prep time: 15 minutes / Cook time: 50 minutes

Root vegetables are available year-round, but this stew is best prepared in late summer and fall when these ingredients are naturally in season. Although stored root vegetables are just fine, their texture can get stringy and their flavor less sweet the longer they sit. The quantity of each vegetable can be varied depending on your palate, and other starchy vegetables can be thrown into the stew. Pumpkin, winter squash, and celeriac would combine well with the other ingredients.

NUT-FREE

VEGAN

1 tablespoon coconut oil
2 leeks, white and light green parts, chopped
2 potatoes, peeled and diced
2 parsnips, peeled and diced
1 sweet potato, peeled and diced
1 large carrot, peeled and diced
6 cups gluten-free vegetable stock
1 tablespoon chopped fresh thyme
1 teaspoon chopped fresh oregano
1 large red bell pepper, diced
2 cups shredded collard greens
Sea salt
Freshly ground black pepper

1. In a large stockpot over medium-high heat, heat the coconut oil.

2. Sauté the leeks until they are softened, about 5 minutes.

3. Add the potatoes, parsnips, sweet potato, carrot, vegetable stock, thyme, and oregano.

4. Bring the stew to a boil; then reduce the heat to low and simmer until the vegetables are tender, about 40 minutes.

5. Stir in the red bell pepper and collard greens, and simmer for 5 minutes more.

6. Season the stew with salt and pepper, and serve.

PER SERVING Calories: 244; Total Fat: 4g; Saturated Fat: 3g; Cholesterol: 0mg; Total Carbohydrates: 48g; Fiber: 11g; Protein: 6g

Chapter Ten
Snacks

Spiced Apple Chips

Serves 4 / Prep time: 10 minutes / Cook time: 2 hours

NUT-FREE

VEGAN

Apples are a nutrient-dense, low-calorie fruit that provides almost every mineral and vitamin in some amount. The best apples to use in any recipe are fall or early winter apples because these are the freshest and sweetest. Apples can be stored year-round in climate-controlled units, but summer apples can be mealy textured because their starch turns to sugar as they sit. If your apples are not crisp, use them for applesauce instead of these simple chips.

2 Granny Smith apples, cored and thinly sliced
Ground cinnamon, for seasoning
Ground nutmeg, for seasoning
Sea salt

1. Preheat the oven to 225°F.
2. Line 2 baking sheets with parchment paper.
3. Spread the apple slices on the baking sheets with no overlap.
4. Sprinkle the slices with the cinnamon, nutmeg, and salt.
5. Bake until the chips are dry, turning several times, about 2 hours.
6. Remove the chips from the oven, and let them cool on the baking sheets.
7. Store the apple chips in a sealed container at room temperature for up to 3 days.

PER SERVING Calories: 47; Total Fat: 0g; Saturated Fat: 0g; Cholesterol: 0mg; Total Carbohydrates: 13g; Fiber: 2g; Protein: 0g

Cinnamon-Pear Leather

Serves 6 / Prep time: 15 minutes / Cook time: 7 hours, 20 minutes

Commercially prepared fruit leathers are so packed with sugar and preservatives, you can't even taste the original fruit base. Homemade fruit leathers burst with flavor, and are low in calories and sugar. Almost any fruit can be successfully made into leather, as well as combinations of fruit and vegetables. Try puréeing cooked parsnip into this recipe for a delicious, nutritious variation.

NUT-FREE

VEGAN

2 pounds ripe Bartlett pears, peeled, cored, and cut into chunks
¼ cup water
1 teaspoon white vinegar
½ teaspoon ground cinnamon
Pinch sea salt

1. Preheat the oven to 170°F.

2. Line a baking sheet with parchment paper; set aside.

3. In a medium saucepan over medium heat, bring the pears, water, vinegar, cinnamon, and salt to a boil; then reduce the heat to low and simmer, stirring occasionally, until the fruit is very tender, about 20 minutes.

4. Transfer the pear mixture to a food processor or blender, and purée until very smooth.

5. Pour the pear mixture onto the baking sheet, and using a spatula, spread it out until very thin.

6. Bake until the fruit leather is slightly sticky to the touch, about 7 hours.

7. Remove the sheet from the oven, and allow the fruit leather to cool completely.

8. Peel the fruit leather off the parchment paper, and transfer it to a cutting board. Using scissors, cut the leather into strips.

9. Store the leather in an airtight container for up to 3 weeks.

PER SERVING Calories: 131; Total Fat: 0g; Saturated Fat: 0g; Cholesterol: 0mg; Total Carbohydrates: 35g; Fiber: 7g; Protein: 1g

Roasted Red Pepper Dip

Serves 4 / Prep time: 30 minutes / Cook time: 20 minutes

If you are seeking a scrumptious dip and versatile sauce, look no further than this glorious-hued red bell pepper creation. Make a double batch; dip vegetables into half as a snack and toss the other half with zucchini noodles as a main course entrée. This dip freezes well for up to 3 months in a sealed container.

NUT-FREE

VEGAN

4 red bell peppers, halved and seeded
2 tablespoons melted coconut oil, divided
2 tablespoons chopped fresh parsley
2 tablespoons chopped fresh basil
1 teaspoon white vinegar
Pinch red pepper flakes
Sea salt
Freshly ground black pepper

1. Preheat the oven to broil.

2. In a large bowl, toss the bell pepper with 1 tablespoon of coconut oil until the vegetables are well coated.

3. Place the peppers, skin-side up, on a baking sheet, and broil them until the skin is lightly charred and the peppers are tender, about 10 minutes.

4. Remove the peppers from the baking sheet to a stainless steel bowl, and cover the bowl tightly with plastic wrap. Let the peppers steam for 10 minutes; then peel the skin off and transfer the skinned peppers to a food processor or blender.

5. Add the remaining 1 tablespoon of coconut oil and the parsley, basil, vinegar, and red pepper flakes to the processor, and pulse until you reach the desired consistency.

6. Season with salt and pepper. Store the dip for up to 1 week in a sealed container in the refrigerator.

PER SERVING Calories: 97; Total Fat: 7g; Saturated Fat: 6g; Cholesterol: 0mg; Total Carbohydrates: 7g; Fiber: 3g; Protein: 1g

Pumpkin Hummus

Serves 4 / Prep time: 15 minutes

Traditional hummus is jazzed up with warm spices and rich puréed pumpkin, creating a savory treat perfect for a family get-together, game night, and as a healthy snack while you curl up with a good book. The sesame seeds add the classic smoky, nutty flavor to this dip along with copper, manganese, and calcium. Fresh roasted pumpkin can be used if you happen to have leftovers from another recipe, as can cooked butternut squash and sweet potato.

NUT-FREE

VEGAN

QUICK & EASY

2 cups canned chickpeas, drained and rinsed

½ cup solid-pack pure pumpkin

2 tablespoons sesame seeds

2 tablespoons melted coconut oil

½ teaspoon grated fresh ginger

¼ teaspoon ground cumin

¼ teaspoon ground nutmeg

Pinch red pepper flakes

Pinch coriander

1. In a food processor or blender, purée the chickpeas, pumpkin, sesame seeds, coconut oil, ginger, cumin, nutmeg, red pepper flakes, and coriander until very smooth, stopping and scraping down the sides at least once.

2. Store the hummus in the refrigerator in a sealed container for up to 1 week.

How It Helps: *Sesame seeds are packed with magnesium, which has been shown to help prevent migraines. Sesame seeds are also very rich in vitamin E, so these little seeds can help prevent migraines triggered by hormones during the menstrual cycle. Vitamin E stabilizes these levels.*

PER SERVING Calories: 242; Total Fat: 13g; Saturated Fat: 7g; Cholesterol: 0mg; Total Carbohydrates: 23g; Fiber: 7g; Protein: 10g

Colorful Veggie Salsa

Serves 4 / Prep time: 30 minutes, plus 1 hour to sit

NUT-FREE

VEGAN

Salsa does not have to be tomato based to be fabulous. The chopping of various vegetables might seem like a great deal of work, but the results are worth the effort. Try to get the vegetables as uniform as possible so that they combine well and you get a little bit of everything in every bite. Salsa can be eaten as a healthy snack scooped onto toasted gluten-free bread or spooned over baked fish as a vibrant topping.

1 English cucumber, peeled and diced small

1 carrot, peeled and diced small

1 red bell pepper, diced small

2 large radishes, diced small

2 scallions, chopped

2 tablespoons chopped fresh cilantro

1 teaspoon white vinegar

Sea salt

Freshly ground black pepper

1. In a large bowl, stir together the cucumber, carrot, bell pepper, radishes, scallions, cilantro, and vinegar until combined.

2. Season the salsa with salt and pepper.

3. Let the salsa sit for an hour to let the flavors combine, and store in the refrigerator for up to 3 days.

PER SERVING Calories: 30; Total Fat: 0g; Saturated Fat: 0g; Cholesterol: 0mg; Total Carbohydrates: 7g; Fiber: 2g; Protein: 1g

Peach Bruschetta

Serves 4 / Prep time: 15 minutes, plus 2 hours to chill

Peaches are a logical substitution for tomatoes in bruschetta because they are colorful, sweet, and juicy. Despite being fruit based, this bruschetta is still savory due to the vinegar and scallion. Choose ripe, firm peaches for the best results. Leave the skin on the fruit, making sure to wash it thoroughly with soapy water if you do not buy organic. Peaches are on the dirty dozen list most years for pesticide contamination.

○ NUT-FREE

○ VEGAN

2 ripe peaches, pitted and diced
½ cup chopped roasted red pepper
1 scallion, chopped
1 tablespoon fresh basil, chopped
1 teaspoon white vinegar
1 teaspoon melted coconut oil
Pinch sea salt
Pinch freshly ground black pepper
8 slices fresh gluten-free baguette, lightly toasted

1. In a medium bowl, stir together the peach, red pepper, scallion, basil, vinegar, coconut oil, salt and pepper.

2. Refrigerate for 2 hours to let the flavors combine.

3. Spoon the bruschetta evenly onto the toasted bread, and serve.

Allergy Adjustment: *If gluten and whole grains do not act as a migraine trigger for you, replace the gluten-free bread with a traditional crusty whole-grain baguette.*

PER SERVING Calories: 175; Total Fat: 2g; Saturated Fat: 1g; Cholesterol: 0mg; Total Carbohydrates: 36g; Fiber: 3g; Protein: 4g

Sweet Potato Fries

Serves 4 / Prep time: 20 minutes / Cook time: 30 minutes

NUT-FREE

VEGAN

Sweet potatoes are one of the greatest sources of beta-carotene, which the body converts to vitamin A. Beta-carotene is a powerful antioxidant that protects the body from disease-causing free radicals. The added fat in this snack, in the form of coconut oil, increases the amount of beta-carotene that is absorbed from the sweet potatoes by the body. Foods that are considered to be antioxidants are an important addition to a migraine-fighting diet because inflammation is an issue in this condition.

4 sweet potatoes, washed and cut into long, roughly ½-inch-thick wedges
2 tablespoons melted coconut oil
Pinch ground cayenne pepper
Sea salt

1. Preheat the oven to 350°F.
2. Line 2 baking sheets with parchment paper.
3. In a medium bowl, toss the sweet potato with the coconut oil and cayenne pepper.
4. Spread the sweet potato on the baking sheets, and bake until tender and browned, about 30 minutes.
5. Allow the fries to cool slightly, toss them in a bowl with salt to season, and serve.

PER SERVING Calories: 236; Total Fat: 7g; Saturated Fat: 6g; Cholesterol: 0mg; Total Carbohydrates: 42g; Fiber: 6g; Protein: 2g

Spicy Calamari

Serves 4 / Prep time: 10 minutes, plus 1 hour to marinate / Cook time: 5 minutes

Calamari is the Italian word for squid, so when searching for the ingredients for this dish, look for squid on the package. Fresh squid provides the best texture and a sweet taste, but flash-frozen squid products are good quality because the cephalopod mollusk is often processed right on the boat within minutes of being caught. If you clean your own squid, make sure you remove the beak from the head and the hard piece of cartilage that runs through the body. Squid is very high in protein, iron, copper, and iodine.

NUT-FREE

1 tablespoon melted coconut oil

1 teaspoon ground cumin

½ teaspoon chili powder

¼ teaspoon ground coriander

4 large squid, cleaned and cut into ½-inch rounds

Freshly ground black pepper

¼ cup chopped fresh cilantro

1. In a medium bowl, stir together the coconut oil, cumin, chili powder, and coriander.

2. Add the squid, and toss to combine.

3. Refrigerate for 1 hour to marinate, stirring several times.

4. Preheat the barbecue or a grill pan on the stove to medium-high heat.

5. Grill the squid, turning several times, until just cooked through, about 5 minutes.

6. Transfer the squid to a bowl, and season with pepper.

7. Serve topped with cilantro.

PER SERVING Calories: 190; Total Fat: 6g; Saturated Fat: 4g; Cholesterol: 369mg; Total Carbohydrates: 6g; Fiber: 0g; Protein: 27g

Desserts

Sweet Grilled Peaches

Serves 4 / Prep time: 10 minutes / Cook time: 5 minutes

If you have never grilled fruit before, the complex, lightly caramelized results will delight and impress you. The peaches should be ripe but not mushy for the best results and the skin left on to provide stability. When picking peaches, choose fruit that gives slightly when pressed gently with your fingertips and has a distinctive sweet scent. Nectarines and apricots are also spectacular when grilled with a little coconut oil and spice.

4 peaches, halved and pitted
1 tablespoon melted coconut oil
½ teaspoon ground cinnamon
Pinch ground cloves
Pinch sea salt
½ cup freshly whipped cream

1. Preheat the barbecue or a grill pan on the stove to medium, and clean the grill very well.

2. Brush the cut edges of the peaches with the coconut oil.

3. Sprinkle the peaches with the cinnamon, cloves, and salt.

4. Grill the peaches, cut-side down, until they are tender and very lightly charred, about 5 minutes.

5. Serve the peaches warm with a tablespoon of whipped cream on each.

Allergy Adjustment: *If lactose creates problems for you, swap the whipped cream for a fluffy whipped coconut cream topping. Scoop off the coconut cream from the top of a can of chilled full-fat coconut milk, and beat it with hand beaters until the perfect texture.*

PER SERVING Calories: 94; Total Fat: 6g; Saturated Fat: 5g; Cholesterol: 10mg; Total Carbohydrates: 10g; Fiber: 2g; Protein: 1g

NUT-FREE

VEGETARIAN

QUICK &
EASY

Poached Pears

Serves 4 / Prep time: 20 minutes / Cook time: 30 minutes

Sublime poached pears are created with patience and a steady hand with the peeler. Every nick and bump on the peeled pear surface will be visible after the fruit is poached, so use long, smooth strokes to take the skin off. For a more complex flavor, add a cinnamon stick to the poaching liquid or a scattering of cloves. Remember to remove them before pouring the reduced sauce over your finished pears. Forelle pears are a lovely choice for poaching because they are small, perfectly bell shaped, have a firm texture, and do not get mushy in the poaching liquid.

NUT-FREE

VEGAN

1 cup water
2 (7g) stevia packets
1 teaspoon pure vanilla extract
4 Forelle pears, carefully peeled and cored

1. In a medium saucepan over medium heat, bring the water, stevia, and vanilla to a boil.

2. Reduce the heat to low so the liquid simmers gently.

3. Carefully add the pears to the simmering liquid, and cover the pot.

4. Poach the pears, turning several times to get all sides in the liquid, until tender, about 20 minutes total.

5. Using a slotted spoon, remove the pears and set aside on a plate.

6. Increase the heat to medium, and bring the poaching liquid back to a boil.

7. Boil until the liquid is reduced by half and syrupy, about 5 minutes.

8. Pour the reduced liquid over the pears, and serve.

PER SERVING Calories: 121; Total Fat: 0g; Saturated Fat: 0g; Cholesterol: 0mg;
Total Carbohydrates: 32g; Fiber: 7g; Protein: 1g

Homemade Applesauce

Serves 4 / Prep time: 10 minutes / Cook time: 30 minutes

A slow cooker is a wonderful, supervision-free method of creating perfect homemade applesauce. If your slow cooker is larger, you might want to double the recipe so you aren't wasting cooking space. Simply throw all the ingredients into the slow cooker, and cook the applesauce on low for about 7 hours. Then mash and serve. If you prefer a smooth-textured applesauce, toss the cooked apples and all the liquid from the slow cooker or saucepan into a food processor or blender and purée completely.

6 Granny Smith apples, peeled, cored, and chopped
½ cup water
1 teaspoon ground cinnamon
2 (7g) stevia packets
¼ teaspoon grated fresh ginger
Pinch sea salt

1. In a medium saucepan over medium heat, bring the apples, water, cinnamon, stevia, ginger, and salt to a boil.

2. Reduce the heat to low, and simmer until the apples are very tender, about 30 minutes.

3. Remove the apples from the heat, and using a fork or a potato masher, mash them until the applesauce is the desired consistency.

4. Adjust the spicing, and serve warm or chilled.

5. Store the applesauce in a sealed container in the refrigerator for up to 1 week.

PER SERVING Calories: 96; Total Fat: 0 g; Saturated Fat: 0g; Cholesterol: 0mg; Total Carbohydrates: 26g; Fiber: 5g; Protein: 1g

Melon Granita

Serves 4 / Prep time: 15 minutes, plus 8 hours to freeze

Granita is the adult version of a snow cone, so expect individual ice crystals rather than a creamy texture. This sweet, coarse-textured treat finds its roots in Italy, where it was originally created using sweetened fruit juices and snow taken from Mount Etna. If you want a smoother texture when serving this cold confection, instead of scraping the frozen fruit mixture, pop it into a food processor or blender and very quickly pulse until the texture resembles sorbet.

○ NUT-FREE

○ VEGAN

2 cups cubed cantaloupe

2 cups cubed watermelon

½ English cucumber, peeled and diced

1 tablespoon chopped fresh mint

1 teaspoon chopped fresh thyme

1. In a food processor or blender, process the cantaloupe, watermelon, cucumber, mint, and thyme until very smooth.

2. Pour the melon mixture into a 9-by-13-inch metal baking dish.

3. Freeze the baking dish for 2 hours.

4. Stir the partially frozen mixture, scraping the sides, and then return the container to the freezer.

5. Scrape the sides and bottom with a fork every hour until it starts to freeze solid, about 6 hours.

6. When you're ready to serve, use a fork to scrape until the mixture is the texture of snow.

7. Store the granita in a sealed container in the freezer for up to 1 month, scraping whenever you want to serve it.

PER SERVING Calories: 48; Total Fat: 0g; Saturated Fat: 0g; Cholesterol: 0mg; Total Carbohydrates: 11g; Fiber: 5g; Protein: 1g

Mango Ice Cream

Serves 4 / Prep time: 10 minutes, plus freezing time

You will need an ice-cream maker to execute this recipe perfectly, but it can be done with just a freezer and blender if that is all you have. Just freeze the mango and cream mixture solid; then transfer it to a blender or a food processor in a solid piece. Pulse until the mixture resembles soft ice cream, and serve immediately. You can only do this once, so only break or cut off as much of the frozen mango mixture as needed.

4 ripe mangos, peeled, pitted, and cut into chunks
¼ cup heavy (whipping) cream
½ teaspoon pure vanilla extract
¼ teaspoon ground nutmeg

1. In a food processor or blender, purée the mango, cream, vanilla, and nutmeg until smooth.

2. Transfer the mixture to an ice-cream maker, and freeze according to the manufacturer's directions.

3. Store the ice cream in the freezer in a sealed container for up to 1 month.

PER SERVING Calories: 173; Total Fat: 3g; Saturated Fat: 2g; Cholesterol: 10mg; Total Carbohydrates: 36g; Fiber: 4g; Protein: 1g

○
NUT-FREE

○
VEGETARIAN

Blueberry Panna Cotta

Serves 4 / Prep time: 20 minutes, plus 3 hours to set / Cook time: 10 minutes

Gelatin is not as scary an ingredient to use as you might think; it is uncomplicated and creates wonderful results. Gelatin leaves or sheets are one of the most common forms of this product and are simply gelatin granules dried into flat sheets. Leaves create a more translucent, clearer end product than powder or liquid gelatin. Make sure you do not place the gelatin leaves in boiling liquid and that you do not leave them in the softening liquid too long, or they will dissolve and be unusable. You can source out gelatin in powder or liquid form as well for this creamy dessert.

NUT-FREE

3 gelatin leaves

¼ cup cold water

2 cups heavy (whipping) cream

1 cup unsweetened rice milk

1 tablespoon stevia

2 teaspoons pure vanilla extract

2 cups blueberries

1. In a small bowl, place the gelatin leaves in the water to soften for about 5 minutes.

2. In a large saucepan over medium heat, whisk together the cream, milk, stevia, and vanilla.

3. Heat until the liquid is scalded (do not boil), about 10 minutes, and remove the cream mixture from the heat.

4. Take the gelatin leaves out of the water, and squeeze out any excess water.

5. Place the leaves in the warm cream mixture, and stir until they are dissolved.

6. Pour the mixture into 4 serving dishes, and chill until set, about 3 hours.

7. Serve topped with fresh blueberries.

PER SERVING Calories: 270; Total Fat: 23g; Saturated Fat: 14g; Cholesterol: 82mg; Total Carbohydrates: 14g; Fiber: 1g; Protein: 4g

Peaches and Cream Ice Pops

Makes 12 popsicles / Prep time: 15 minutes, plus 3 to 4 hours to freeze / Cook time: 5 minutes

Scorching summer days demand an icy treat to cool and delight. Almost every department store sells ice pop molds in different colors, shapes, and sizes, so homemade was never easier. Strawberries, blueberries, mangos, or nectarines can replace the peaches. You can even add little chopped up bits of fruit to the finished puréed mixture to create some interesting texture in your ice pops. If calories are a concern, cut or replace the heavy cream with rice milk for a lower-calorie option. The ice pops will still be delicious.

4 large ripe peaches, peeled, pitted, and diced
2 tablespoons water
1 cup heavy (whipping) cream
1 teaspoon pure vanilla extract
¼ teaspoon ground cinnamon

1. In a small saucepan over medium-high heat, cook the peaches in the water until the fruit has softened, about 5 minutes.

2. Transfer the cooked peaches to a blender, and purée until smooth.

3. Add the cream, vanilla, and cinnamon, and purée until smooth.

4. Pour the mixture into ice pop molds and freeze until very firm, 3 to 4 hours.

5. Serve.

PER SERVING Calories: 47; Total Fat: 4g; Saturated Fat: 2g; Cholesterol: 14mg; Total Carbohydrates: 4g; Fiber: 1g; Protein: 1g

Honeydew-Mint Ice Pops

Makes 12 / Prep time: 20 minutes

Honeydew melon is often overlooked because its brighter counterparts, watermelon and cantaloupe, steal the culinary spotlight, but honeydew is very high in vitamins B$_6$ and C as well as iron, potassium, and fiber. The trouble with honeydew is that when you get an unripe melon, it tastes unpleasant, and choosing a ripe product can be a challenge. When buying this pretty pale green melon, hold it to your nose. If you can't smell the melon fragrance, it isn't ripe.

NUT-FREE

VEGAN

1 honeydew melon, seeded, peeled, and cut into chunks
½ English cucumber, cut into chunks
¼ cup fresh mint
1 (7g) stevia packet
¼ teaspoon chopped fresh thyme

1. In a food processor or blender, pulse the honeydew, cucumber, mint, stevia, and thyme until the mixture is very smooth.

2. Pour the mixture into ice pop molds and freeze until very firm, 3 to 4 hours.

3. Serve.

PER SERVING Calories: 41; Total Fat: 0g; Saturated Fat: 0g; Cholesterol: 0mg; Total Carbohydrates: 10g; Fiber: 1g; Protein: 1g

Blueberry Cobbler

Serves 4 / Prep time: 25 minutes / Cook time: 40 minutes

Xanthan gum is a thickener and stabilizer used extensively in gluten-free baking. It is plant based and low calorie but can be high in sodium, although not in the small amount used in this recipe. Xanthan gum ensures that the topping will hold together in crispy clumps on the bubbling filling rather than break down into a grainy mess. You can find xanthan gum in most organic or specialty food sections in the grocery store.

FOR THE FILLING
1 teaspoon melted coconut oil, for greasing
2 cups fresh blueberries
1 tablespoon arrowroot powder
½ teaspoon stevia
½ teaspoon ground cinnamon

FOR THE TOPPING
½ cup rice flour
½ cup sweet sorghum flour
1 teaspoon baking powder
½ teaspoon xanthan gum
2 (7g) stevia packets
¼ teaspoon sea salt
2 tablespoons cold coconut oil
½ cup heavy (whipping) cream

TO MAKE THE FILLING

1. Lightly oil an 8-by-8-inch baking dish with coconut oil.

2. In a medium bowl, toss together the blueberries, arrowroot, stevia, and cinnamon.

3. Transfer the berry mixture to the baking dish, and set aside.

TO MAKE THE TOPPING

1. Preheat the oven to 375°F.

2. In a medium bowl, whisk together the rice flour, sorghum flour, baking powder, xanthan gum, stevia, and salt.

3. Cut the coconut oil into the flour mixture until it resembles coarse crumbs.

4. Stir in the cream with a fork until the dough holds together and is uniform.

5. Drop the batter onto the berries by tablespoons; there will be gaps in the topping.

6. Bake the cobbler until the topping is firm and golden and the blueberries are bubbly, about 35 to 40 minutes, and serve.

PER SERVING Calories: 290; Total Fat: 13g; Saturated Fat: 9g; Cholesterol: 21mg; Total Carbohydrates: 40g; Fiber: 4g; Protein: 4g

Apple Crisp

Serves 4 / Prep time: 20 minutes / Cook time: 45 minutes

Read your oat package label carefully because manufacturers package different products in the same plant, and the oats might be contaminated with grains from the same processing area. Oats are naturally gluten-free and are often part of a gluten-free diet like the migraine diet. Oats are very high in fiber, manganese, phosphorus, and copper. They support a healthy cardiovascular system and can help lower blood sugar. Make sure you do not purchase instant oats for this recipe because large flake or rolled oats will provide texture to the topping.

2 tablespoons melted coconut oil, plus more for greasing
5 Granny Smith apples, peeled, cored, and sliced
2 tablespoons arrowroot powder
1 cup gluten-free oats
½ teaspoon ground cinnamon
½ teaspoon ground nutmeg
Pinch ground allspice
Pinch salt

1. Preheat the oven to 350°F.

2. Lightly grease a 9-by-9-inch baking pan with coconut oil.

3. In a medium bowl, toss the apple slices with arrowroot, and transfer them to the baking dish.

4. In a medium bowl, stir together the oats, cinnamon, nutmeg, allspice, salt, and coconut oil until the mixture resembles coarse crumbs.

5. Top the apples with the oatmeal mixture, and cover the dish with foil.

6. Bake, covered, for 30 minutes.

7. Remove the foil, and bake for an additional 15 minutes until the topping is lightly browned.

8. Serve warm.

Allergy Adjustment: *Nuts can be a migraine trigger, but if you can eat them, a ½ cup of chopped pecans is scrumptious in the topping of this crisp. Add them to the oat mixture, and enjoy.*

PER SERVING Calories: 272; Total Fat: 9g; Saturated Fat: 6g; Cholesterol: 0 mg; Total Carbohydrates: 48g; Fiber: 8g; Protein: 4g

Rice Pudding with Berries

Serves 4 / Prep time: 10 minutes / Cook time: 40 minutes

Rice pudding is a versatile dessert that is served with equal success in four-star restaurants and in truck-stop diners. Warm, cold, topped with fruit, or adorned with an intricate pulled-sugar garnish, this pudding holds its own. If you do not have issues with maple syrup or agave nectar, try using a drizzle instead of stevia for a lovely variation. If you'd prefer a thinner-textured pudding, add ½ cup of rice milk to the cooking rice or use extra rice milk to top the pudding before serving.

NUT-FREE

VEGAN

1 vanilla bean, split
2 cups unsweetened rice milk
1 cup white rice
3 (7g) stevia packets
½ teaspoon ground cinnamon
Pinch ground allspice
Pinch sea salt
2 cups mixed berries (strawberries and blueberries)

1. In a medium saucepan over medium-high heat, using the tip of a paring knife, scrape the vanilla beans into the rice milk.

2. Add the empty vanilla bean pod to the milk, and bring the mixture to a simmer.

3. Reduce the heat to low, and simmer for 10 minutes to infuse.

4. Remove the vanilla bean from the milk, and add the rice, stevia, cinnamon, allspice, and salt to milk.

5. Increase the heat to medium and cook, stirring frequently, until the rice is tender and has absorbed most of the liquid, about 30 minutes.

6. Serve the rice pudding warm topped with the berries.

PER SERVING Calories: 270; Total Fat: 2g; Saturated Fat: 0g; Cholesterol: 0mg; Total Carbohydrates: 58g; Fiber: 3g; Protein: 4g

Crustless Pumpkin Cheesecake

Serves 4 / Prep time: 20 minutes

Texture is a crucial consideration in cooking, especially in desserts and sauces. The added whipped cream creates a tantalizing mousse texture in this dish. The trick is to fold the whipped cream very carefully to retain as much volume as possible. If you just stir it into the pumpkin mixture, the taste will still be lovely, but you will miss out on the melt-in-your-mouth experience.

NUT-FREE

VEGETARIAN

QUICK & EASY

8 ounces cream cheese, softened

1 cup solid-pack pure pumpkin

1 tablespoon stevia

½ teaspoon ground cinnamon

¼ teaspoon ground nutmeg

Pinch ground cloves

1 cup heavy (whipping) cream

1. In a large bowl, beat together the cream cheese, pumpkin, stevia, cinnamon, nutmeg, and cloves with a hand beater until fluffy and very well blended.

2. In a medium bowl, beat the cream until soft peaks form; fold the whipped cream into the cream cheese mixture.

3. Spoon the pumpkin cheesecake into 4 serving bowls, and refrigerate until you wish to serve it.

PER SERVING Calories: 324; Total Fat: 31g; Saturated Fat: 20g; Cholesterol: 103mg; Total Carbohydrates: 8g; Fiber: 2g; Protein: 6g

Kitchen Staples

Barbecue Spice Rub

Makes ½ cup / Prep time: 5 minutes

Having an all-purpose spice blend that works with red meat, chicken, pork, seafood, and vegetables is convenient for times when you want a quick grilled meal. There is no added salt in this blend because the celery salt adds that flavor, and celery is naturally salty. Smoked paprika would work for just a meat and poultry blend, and coriander would be a nice addition for seafood and vegetable dishes. Since the spice mix keeps well in a sealed container, double or triple the recipe so you always have some on hand.

NUT-FREE

VEGAN

QUICK &
EASY

2 tablespoons celery salt

2 tablespoons dried oregano

2 tablespoons dried thyme

1 teaspoon freshly ground black pepper

½ teaspoon dried marjoram

½ teaspoon ground paprika

½ teaspoon ground coriander

1. In a small bowl, stir together the celery salt, oregano, thyme, pepper, marjoram, paprika, and coriander until well combined.

2. Transfer the spice mixture to a sealed container, and store it in a cool dark place for up to 2 months.

PER SERVING (1 tablespoon) Calories: 7; Total Fat: 0g; Saturated Fat: 0g; Cholesterol: 0mg; Total Carbohydrates: 2g; Fiber: 1g; Protein: 0g

Herb Pesto

Makes 2 cups / Prep time: 15 minutes

Pesto can be created using a plethora of ingredients ranging from sun-dried tomatoes and olives to herbs and dark leafy greens. This version is herb based with a hint of acid from the vinegar and a touch of salt. The amounts of herbs are only a guideline, so adjust the ingredients until you have a combination that pleases you. Pesto can be added to many recipes such as stews, soups, and sauces for flavor, and it makes a tasty topping on grilled fish and poultry. Try a spoon tossed into gluten-free pasta when you need a quick dinner or lunch.

1 cup fresh basil
½ cup fresh oregano
½ cup fresh mint
2 teaspoons white vinegar
½ cup melted coconut oil
Sea salt

NUT-FREE

VEGAN

QUICK & EASY

1. In a blender, pulse the basil, oregano, mint, and vinegar until the mixture is very finely chopped.

2. Drizzle in the coconut oil in a thin stream while the blender is running until all the oil is used up.

3. Stop, scrape down the sides of the blender, season with salt, and pulse until the pesto is the desired texture.

4. Store the pesto in a sealed container in the refrigerator up to 2 weeks.

Allergy Adjustment: *If olive oil is not a migraine trigger for you, use it in place of the coconut oil for this pesto. Extra-virgin olive oil is packed with migraine-fighting omega-3 fatty acids.*

PER SERVING (2 tablespoons) Calories: 67; Total Fat: 7g; Saturated Fat: 6g; Cholesterol: 0mg; Total Carbohydrates: 2g; Fiber: 1g; Protein: 0g

Date Paste Sweetener

Makes 1 cup / Prep time: 15 minutes, plus overnight to soak

NUT-FREE

VEGAN

Sugar and any other sweetener besides stevia can be a migraine trigger, so creating a natural alternative is important—especially if you have a sweet tooth. Dates are the perfect base for a sweetener because they contain 63 grams of sugar per 100 grams of dates. Dates do not adversely impact blood sugar despite their high sugar content and are considered a low-glycemic food. Dates are high in fiber and potassium, so they support the digestive system and cardiovascular health.

8 ounces pitted dates
½ cup water
½ vanilla bean
Pinch sea salt

1. In a medium bowl, refrigerate the dates in the water overnight to soak.

2. Transfer the dates and water to a blender, and using the tip of a paring knife, scrape the seeds from the vanilla bean into the blender with the salt.

3. Purée until the mixture is very smooth, about 5 minutes.

4. Store the paste in a sealed container in the refrigerator for up to 1 month.

PER SERVING (1 tablespoon) Calories: 40; Total Fat: 0g; Saturated Fat: 0g; Cholesterol: 0mg; Total Carbohydrates: 11g; Fiber: 1g; Protein: 0g

Simple Chicken Stock

Makes 8 cups / Prep time: 15 minutes / Cook time: 12 hours

Commercially prepared stock can contain gluten and MSG, as well as lots of sodium and harmful additives, so making your own should be high on your priority list when trying to control migraines. This simple recipe can be a once-a-month project to ensure you have stock on hand for your cooking needs. Freeze the stock in containers or even in ice cube trays.

NUT-FREE

2 chicken carcasses

4 shallots, crushed

2 carrots, peeled and roughly chopped

2 celery stalks, quartered

4 fresh thyme sprigs

2 bay leaves

1 teaspoon black peppercorns

1. Preheat the oven to 350°F.

2. Place the chicken carcasses in a baking pan, and roast them for 30 minutes.

3. Transfer the carcasses to a large stockpot, and add the shallots, carrots, celery, thyme, bay leaves, peppercorns, and enough water to cover the ingredients by 3 inches.

4. Place the stockpot on high heat, and bring to a boil.

5. Reduce the heat to low, and gently simmer the chicken bone broth, stirring every few hours, for 12 hours. Remove the pot from the heat, and cool for 15 minutes.

6. Using tongs, remove any large chicken bones; then strain the broth through a fine-mesh sieve and discard the solid bits.

7. Pour the stock into containers or jars, and cool it completely.

8. Store the stock in sealed containers or jars in the refrigerator for up to 5 days, or in the freezer for up to 3 months.

PER SERVING (1 cup) Calories: 30; Total Fat: 3g; Saturated Fat: 1g; Cholesterol: 0mg; Total Carbohydrates: 0g; Fiber: 0g; Protein: 1g

Dark Beef Stock

Makes 8 cups / Prep time: 15 minutes / Cook time: 24 hours

NUT-FREE

Roasting the beef bones before making stock creates a deeper, richer flavor, and a lovely dark-colored liquid. If you want a lighter, more delicate tasting broth rather than a stock, do not roast the bones and only simmer the ingredients for about 1 hour before straining the solids out. Shorter cooking time will reduce the amount of nutrients and flavor in the liquid. Beef broth can be stored in the same manner as beef stock.

2 pounds beef bones
3 shallots, lightly crushed
2 carrots, peeled and roughly chopped
2 celery stalks, cut into chunks
4 fresh thyme sprigs
½ cup fresh parsley
3 bay leaves
1 teaspoon black peppercorns

1. Preheat the oven to 350°F.
2. Place the beef bones in a baking pan, and roast them for 30 minutes.
3. Transfer the roasted bones to a large stockpot, and add the shallots, carrots, celery, thyme, parsley, bay leaves, peppercorns, and enough water to cover all the ingredients by 3 inches.
4. Place the pot on high heat, and bring to a boil.
5. Reduce the heat to low, and simmer the stock for 24 hours.

6. Check the broth every half hour for the first 3 hours to skim off the top with a spoon.

7. Remove the stockpot from the heat, and cool for 15 minutes.

8. Using tongs, remove any large beef bones; then strain the stock through a fine-mesh sieve and discard the solid bits.

9. Pour the stock into containers or jars, and allow it to cool completely.

10. Store the stock in sealed containers or jars in the refrigerator for up to 5 days, or in the freezer for up to 3 months.

PER SERVING (1 cup) Calories: 80; Total Fat: 5g; Saturated Fat: 1g; Cholesterol: 0mg; Total Carbohydrates: 0g; Fiber: 0g; Protein: 4g

Tips for Eating Out

Whether you are in the elimination stage or the long-term maintenance phase of the *Migraine Relief Diet*, you may be wondering how you can enjoy meals at restaurants—if at all. The good news is that you will not have to refuse every dinner invitation from here on out.

Food allergies are becoming increasingly common in society, and restaurants have therefore become accustomed to dealing with individual customer requests. The following tips will show you how easy it is to dine out while sticking to the principles of your new style of eating.

Do your research. If you know which restaurant you will be dining at in advance, plan ahead. Visit the restaurant's website to see if they offer nutritional or allergen information online, and select a dish accordingly. Alternatively, call to make sure they are able to cater to your requests. It is also often easier for the wait staff to communicate with the chef if you call during a quiet time of day rather than during the busy mealtime rush.

Be selective with your choice of restaurant. Sometimes this is out of your control but, where possible, try to eat at larger and more established restaurants, as they will generally have more experience in catering to their customers' needs. Chain restaurants are also more likely to have their nutritional information available online.

Befriend your server. Be kind to your server and explain your dietary requirements. Phrase your sensitivities as "allergies," and they will likely endeavor to do everything in their control to prevent you from falling ill. If the staff provides particularly good service, reward them by leaving a generous tip.

Don't be afraid to ask. If you do not see anything on the menu that caters to your dietary needs, try ordering off-menu. Even if such a dish is not listed on the menu, most restaurants will be able to prepare steak, chicken, or fish without added seasonings, accompanied by fresh vegetables.

Remember that simple is best. Keep the more complicated meals for at home, where you can prepare them yourself with no added surprises.

Visit favorites on rotation. Once you have eaten at a few restaurants that have happily accommodated your needs, you can build up a nice rotation of favorite restaurants. Provided you left a good tip as suggested above, they will likely remember your special requirements and will be happy to assist you again in the future.

Avoid eating at peak times. It is much easier for a restaurant to make recommendations and ensure your food does not contain allergenic ingredients if they are not dealing with a busy, full dining room. If you are going out for dinner, try eating before 6 p.m. or after 9 p.m.

Speak to everyone, if necessary. If you feel that your server is not taking your allergy seriously, or if they are uncertain about the ingredients of a particular dish, ask to speak to the manager or chef personally. If your instinct still tells you that something is off, do not be afraid to leave and go elsewhere.

Consider a backup plan. If you call in advance and discover that the restaurant in question does not serve anything suitable for your consumption, and you have no choice but to attend the meal anyway, eat ahead of time and simply enjoy a beverage while the rest of your dining party eats.

Never get caught out. Sometimes you might find yourself out all day, to wind up starving with only unsuitable restaurants to choose from. Instead of eating highly allergenic foods and risking triggering a migraine, always keep snacks handy to tide you over until you can find a better option or make it home.

Where to Shop

Where possible, it is best to buy organic meat, fruits, and vegetables. This may not always be easy to do in a regular grocery store, so it may be best to seek out one of the following options.

Farmers' Markets

Farmers' markets are stocked with a large variety of fresh, local, and seasonal produce. Most farmers at such markets use organic methods to grow their produce, which means you will be purchasing a higher quality of food. The bonus is that, unlike in regular grocery stores, the organic fruits and vegetables at farmers' markets are rarely more expensive than their conventionally grown alternatives. Furthermore, by shopping at farmers' markets you will support the local economy.

CSAs (Community Supported Agriculture)

CSAs, or community supported agriculture, are programs whereby you purchase "shares" in a local farm in exchange for weekly deliveries of fruits, vegetables, and other farm products such as eggs, milk, butter, and honey. Being part of a CSA program can help increase your creativity by supplying you with produce you may

not have otherwise purchased, and it can also help keep you motivated to cook rather than eat out, as you will be less inclined to waste food you already have at home.

Local harvest (localharvest.org) is an online resource for finding your closest farmers' markets and CSA programs. The website provides information about each farm's history, season, and crops, and also includes customer reviews.

Co-ops and Farm Stands

Natural food co-ops offer an affordable way to seek out organic produce local to you. A great online resource is the Co-op Directory (coopdirectory.org), which allows you to search directories and distributors.

Farm stands are found in farmers' markets. The Farmstead App (farmstandapp.com) helps you find information and pictures from more than 8,700 markets worldwide. Eating local, nutritious food is as simple as downloading an app to your smartphone!

Organic Meats and Seafood

By eating organic meat from naturally raised animals, you avoid being exposed to the hormones, antibiotics, pesticides, and chemicals that are pumped into conventionally raised animals. The best options are grass-fed beef, free-range poultry, wild-caught fish, and pastured pork.

Where possible, it is best to eat meats that are clearly labeled as both pastured and organic. If you do not have a produce market near you, seek out organic and pastured meat and fish using one of the following resources.

EatWild.Com. This online database contains information on more than 1,400 ranchers across the United States and Canada that sell organic pastured meats and eggs. Each listing contains the farm's selling conditions; some sell entire animals in bulk, while others allow individual pieces to be purchased.

Get Maine Lobster. Get Maine Lobster (GetMaineLobster.com) delivers both fresh and live lobster, as well as other seafood, direct from Portland, Maine. Overnight shipping to all states is available.

Tendergrass Farms. Tendergrass Farms (Tendergrass.com) is another online supplier that ships a wide variety of organic meat products throughout the United States.

U.S. Wellness Meats. This online meat retailer (GrasslandBeef.com) offers a wide variety of high-quality pastured animal products for frozen delivery. The website also contains a recipe database to help inspire you in the kitchen.

Wild Pacific Salmon. Wild Pacific Salmon (WildPacificSalmon.com) offers wild salmon and other seafood for delivery throughout the United States. All of the produce is caught in Alaska, Canada, and the Pacific Northwest.

Resources

The following list of additional resources provides more information about migraines.

The Alliance for Headache Disorders Advocacy is a nonprofit organization dedicated to finding better treatments for all headache disorder patients. info@headacheadvocacy.org. www.allianceforheadacheadvocacy.org.

The American Council for Headache Education is another nonprofit organization that provides educational resources concerning the mechanisms and treatment of headaches to health care providers. achehq@talley.com. www.achenet.org. tel: 856-423-0258.

The American Headache Society is a professional society of health care providers who are dedicated to the study and treatment of headache and face pain. ahshq@talley.com. www.americanheadachesociety.org. tel: 856-423-0043.

The Association of Migraine Disorders was founded by otolaryngologists—Drs. Frederick Godley and Michael Teixido—who recognized that migraineurs often suffer other neurological symptoms that do not include a headache. info@migrainedisorders.org. www.migrainedisorders.org.

Headache and Migraine News is a website that contains all the latest news about migraines, cluster headaches, and treatment options around the world. www.headacheandmigrainenews.com.

The Migraine Research Foundation website provides a directory of all the doctors within the United States who specialize in migraines and headaches. This resource can be found at www.migraineresearchfoundation.org/diplomates.html.

Migraine.com features articles, discussion boards, and polls concerning migraines and headaches. www.migraine.com.

MigraineCast is a weekly podcast that provides information and support for migraineurs. www.migrainecast.com.

The National Headache Foundation was founded to both increase awareness of headache and migraine as legitimate neurobiological diseases and encourage research into potential causes and treatment options. info@headaches.org. www.headaches.org. tel: 888-643-5552.

The National Institute of Neurological Disorders and Stroke has a mission of reducing the burden of neurological disease by seeking fundamental knowledge about the brain and nervous system. www.ninds.nih.gov/disorders/migraine/migraine.htm. tel: 800-352-9424.

References

American Headache Society. "Epidemiology and Impact of Headache and Migraine." Accessed September 18, 2015. www. americanheadachesociety.org/assets/ 1/7/NAP_for_Web_-_Epidemiology__ Impact_of_Headache__Migraine.pdf.

Cady, R.K., K. Farmer, J.K. Dexter, and J. Hall. "The Bowel and Migraine: Update on Celiac Disease and Inflammatory Bowel Disease." *Curr Pain Headache Rep 16*, no. 3 (June 2012): 278–286.

Celiac Central. "Non-Celiac Gluten Sensitivity." Accessed September 22, 2015. www.celiaccentral.org/ non-celiac-gluten-sensitivity/.

Centers for Disease Control and Prevention. "Ambulatory Health Care Data." Accessed September 4, 2015. www.cdc.gov/nchs/ahcd.htm/.

Collective Evolution. "Most Human Beings are Lactose Intolerant: Here's Why." Accessed October 17, 2015. www. collective-evolution.com/2013/04/03/ over-75-of-earths-population-is-lactose-intolerant-for-a-reason-dairy-is-harmful/.

EatRight Ontario. "The Truth About Nitrates." Accessed September 9, 2015. www.eatrightontario.ca/en/Articles/ Food-technology/Biotechnology/Novel-foods/The-truth-about-nitrates.aspx/.

Fallon, Sally and Mary G. Enig. "Inside Japan: Surprising Facts About Japanese Foodways." January 1, 2000. www.westonaprice.org/ health-topics/inside-japan-surprising-facts-about-japanese-foodways/#sthash. 0S8K0p4R.dpuf.

Life Enhancement. "Coenzyme Q10 Helps Prevent Migraine." Accessed October 16, 2015. www.life-enhancement.com/ magazine/article/1072-coenzyme-q10-helps-prevent-migraine/.

Life Extension. "Preventing Migraine Pain with Butterbur." Accessed October 16, 2015. www.lifeextension.com/magazine/2008/8/ Preventing-Migraine-Pain-with-Butterbur/ Page-01/.

Lipton, R.B., W.F. Stewart, S. Diamond, M.L. Diamond, and M. Reed. "Prevalence and Burden of Migraine in the United States: Data From the American Migraine Study II." *Headache: The Journal of Head and Face Pain* 41, no. 7 (July 2001): 646–657.

Magnesium Online Resource Center. "Understanding What Causes Migraine Headaches, Depression, Insomnia, and Bipolar Symptoms and Signs." Accessed October 16, 2015. www.mg12.info/articles/ migraine-headache.html/.

Marcus, D.A., L. Scharff, D. Turk, and L.M. Gourley. "A Double-Blind Provocative Study of Chocolate as a Trigger of Headache." *Cephalalgia* 17, no. 8 (December 1997): 855–62.

Migraine.com. "Feverfew for the Treatment of Migraine Headaches: An Introduction." Accessed October 16, 2015. migraine.com/migraine-treatment/natural-remedies/feverfew/.

———. "Ginger for the Treatment of Migraine Headaches: An Introduction." Accessed September 21, 2015. migraine.com/migraine-treatment/natural-remedies/ginger-for-migraine-headaches/.

———. "Migraine Statistics." Accessed July 12, 2015. http://migraine.com/migraine-statistics/.

———. "Migraines in Children and Teens." Accessed October 25, 2015. migraine.com/migraines-in-children-and-teens/.

The Migraine Trust. "Menstruation and Migraine." Accessed September 18, 2015. www.migrainetrust.org/factsheet-menstruation-and-migraine-10883/.

National Headache Foundation. "Chocolate: Headache Friend or Foe?" Accessed September 22, 2015. www.headaches.org/2009/10/02/chocolate-headache-friend-or-foe/.

Pribila, B.A., S.R. Hertzler, B.R. Martin, C.M. Weaver, and D.A. Savaiano. "Improved Lactose Digestion and Intolerance Among African-American Adolescent Girls Fed a Dairy Rich Diet." *Journal of the Academy of Nutrition and Dietetics* 100, no. 5 (May 2000): 524–528.

Rees, T., D. Watson, S. Lipscombe, H. Speight, P. Cousins, G. Hardman, and A. Dowson. "A Prospective Audit of Food Intolerance Among Migraine Patients in Primary Care Clinical Practice." *Headache Care* 2, no. 1 (June 2005): 11–14.

Samsel, A. "Obesity, Corn, GMOs." Accessed September 22, 2015. www.cornucopia.org/2012/07/obesity-corn-gmos/.

Smitherman, T.A., R. Burch, H. Sheikh, and E. Loder. "The Prevalence, Impact, and Treatment of Migraine and Severe Headaches in the United States: A Review of Statistics from National Surveillance Studies." *Headache: The Journal of Head and Face Pain* 53 (March 2013): 427–436.

———. "Vitamins for Migraine - 2007." Accessed October 16, 2015. *www.migrainetrust.org/research-article-vitamins-for-migraine-2007-11209/.*

WebMD. "Feverfew." Accessed October 16, 2015. www.webmd.com/vitamins-supplements/ingredientmono-933-feverfew.id=933&activeingredientname=feverfew/.

Recipe Index

Index

About the Author

As a qualified nutritionist and personal trainer, **Tara Spencer** works to guide people on their path toward good health. She is experienced with eating disorder recovery, athlete coaching, and utilizing diet as a natural treatment method for a number of illnesses. Her work as a nutritionist has given her the opportunity to impact a wide range of people of all ages and stages, from novice bodybuilding competitors to professional tennis players. To learn more about Tara, visit her online at www.sweatlikeapig.com.

About the Foreword Authors

Dr. Frederick Godley is a general otolaryngologist at University Otolaryngology and is president of the Association of Migraine Disorders, a nonprofit organization devoted to migraine awareness, education, and research. He attended Boston University Medical School, completed his specialty training at Yale–New Haven Hospital, and served on the teaching staff at Johns Hopkins Hospital before moving to Rhode Island.

Dr. Michael Teixido is an otolaryngologist with an active neurotologic practice at ENT & Allergy of Delaware and is vice president of the Association of Migraine Disorders. He attended medical school at Wake Forest University and completed his specialty training at Loyola University Medical Center. He is the director of the Delaware Otologic Medicine and Surgery Fellowship, director of the Balance and Mobility Center of Christiana Care, and co-director of the Pediatric Cochlear Implant and Auditory Rehabilitation Program of the duPont Hospital for Children.

CPSIA information can be obtained
at www.ICGtesting.com
Printed in the USA
BVHW021930260220
573416BV00010B/14

9 781623 159498